WORKING WITH

MANAGEMENT

PACKS

Using VB.Net and JScript

Richard Thomas Edwards

CONTENTS

Creating a Management Pack...3
The crude but bare Bones Management Pack 15

    REFERENCES 17
    Classes 21
    The Discovery 23
    Views and Folders..31
    Language Packs and Display Strings..32

SQL Server and the SRS Report 37
The HTML Report 81
Stylesheets 82

    NONE...82
    BLACK AND WHITE TEXT 82
    COLORED TEXT 85
    OSCILLATING ROW COLORS 87
    GHOST DECORATED 90
    3D 92
    SHADOW BOX...98

Creating a Management Pack

If you are like me, chances are good you have either had to either use the authoring tool or hand write a Management Pack. Either way, the Management Pack (MP). Management to work the way you wanted but it was a slow, a totally vertical learning curve and an experience you don't plan on doing again.

Well, take heart, you are not alone. There are literally thousands of you who have worked with custom MPs and you have discovered through the school of hard knots that the blood, sweat and tears doesn't stop with the creation of the MP, it's the SRS reports, the tweaking and the onboarding. The combination of all of the above adding is own varieties of a discomfort.

What if you could automate the process of creating MPs to the point where your efforts would far exceed your costs? What if you could produce an MP like this:

```
<ManagementPack ContentReadable="true"
xmlns:xsd="http://www.w3.org/2001/XMLSchema"
xmlns:xsl="http://www.w3.org/1999/XSL/Transform">
    <Manifest>
     <Identity>
      <ID>PlanetMPs.Win32_BIOS.ManagementPack</ID>
      <Version>1.0.0.0</Version>
     </Identity>
     <Name>PlanetMPs Win32_BIOS ManagementPack</Name>
     <References>
      <Reference Alias="System">
       <ID>System.Library</ID>
```

```xml
      <Version>6.0.4941.0</Version>
      <PublicKeyToken>31bf3856ad364e35</PublicKeyToken>
    </Reference>
    <Reference Alias="Health">
     <ID>System.Health.Library</ID>
     <Version>6.0.4941.0</Version>
     <PublicKeyToken>31bf3856ad364e35</PublicKeyToken>
    </Reference>
    <Reference Alias="Perf">
     <ID>System.Performance.Library</ID>
     <Version>6.0.4941.0</Version>
     <PublicKeyToken>31bf3856ad364e35</PublicKeyToken>
    </Reference>
    <Reference Alias="Windows">
     <ID>Microsoft.Windows.Library</ID>
     <Version>6.0.4941.0</Version>
     <PublicKeyToken>31bf3856ad364e35</PublicKeyToken>
    </Reference>
    <Reference Alias="SC">
     <ID>Microsoft.SystemCenter.Library</ID>
     <Version>6.0.4941.0</Version>
     <PublicKeyToken>31bf3856ad364e35</PublicKeyToken>
    </Reference>
   </References>
  </Manifest>
  <TypeDefinitions>
   <EntityTypes>
    <ClassTypes>
     <ClassType ID="PlanetMPs.Win32_BIOS.Class" Accessibility="Internal"
Abstract="false" Base="Windows!Microsoft.Windows.LocalApplication"
Hosted="true" Singleton="false">
       <Property ID="BiosCharacteristics" Type="string" Key="false" />
       <Property ID="BIOSVersion" Type="string" Key="false" />
       <Property ID="BuildNumber" Type="string" Key="false" />
       <Property ID="Caption" Type="string" Key="false" />
       <Property ID="CodeSet" Type="string" Key="false" />
       <Property ID="CurrentLanguage" Type="string" Key="false" />
       <Property ID="Description" Type="string" Key="false" />
       <Property ID="IdentificationCode" Type="string" Key="false" />
       <Property ID="InstallableLanguages" Type="string" Key="false" />
```

```xml
            <Property ID="InstallDate" Type="string" Key="false" />
            <Property ID="LanguageEdition" Type="string" Key="false" />
            <Property ID="ListOfLanguages" Type="string" Key="false" />
            <Property ID="Manufacturer" Type="string" Key="false" />
            <Property ID="Name" Type="string" Key="false" />
            <Property ID="OtherTargetOS" Type="string" Key="false" />
            <Property ID="PrimaryBIOS" Type="string" Key="false" />
            <Property ID="ReleaseDate" Type="string" Key="false" />
            <Property ID="SerialNumber" Type="string" Key="false" />
            <Property ID="SMBIOSBIOSVersion" Type="string" Key="false" />
            <Property ID="SMBIOSMajorVersion" Type="string" Key="false" />
            <Property ID="SMBIOSMinorVersion" Type="string" Key="false" />
            <Property ID="SMBIOSPresent" Type="string" Key="false" />
            <Property ID="SoftwareElementID" Type="string" Key="false" />
            <Property ID="SoftwareElementState" Type="string" Key="false" />
            <Property ID="Status" Type="string" Key="false" />
            <Property ID="TargetOperatingSystem" Type="string" Key="false" />
            <Property ID="Version" Type="string" Key="false" />
          </ClassType>
        </ClassTypes>
      </EntityTypes>
    </TypeDefinitions>
    <Monitoring>
      <Discoveries>
        <Discovery ID="PlanetMPs.Win32_BIOS.Class.Discovery" Enabled="true"
Target="Windows!Microsoft.Windows.Computer" ConfirmDelivery="false"
Remotable="true" Priority="Normal">
          <Category>Discovery</Category>
          <DiscoveryTypes>
            <DiscoveryClass TypeID="PlanetMPs.Win32_BIOS.Class">
              <Property PropertyID="BiosCharacteristics" />
              <Property PropertyID="BIOSVersion" />
              <Property PropertyID="BuildNumber" />
              <Property PropertyID="Caption" />
              <Property PropertyID="CodeSet" />
              <Property PropertyID="CurrentLanguage" />
              <Property PropertyID="Description" />
              <Property PropertyID="IdentificationCode" />
              <Property PropertyID="InstallableLanguages" />
              <Property PropertyID="InstallDate" />
```

```
            <Property PropertyID="LanguageEdition" />
            <Property PropertyID="ListOfLanguages" />
            <Property PropertyID="Manufacturer" />
            <Property PropertyID="Name" />
            <Property PropertyID="OtherTargetOS" />
            <Property PropertyID="PrimaryBIOS" />
            <Property PropertyID="ReleaseDate" />
            <Property PropertyID="SerialNumber" />
            <Property PropertyID="SMBIOSBIOSVersion" />
            <Property PropertyID="SMBIOSMajorVersion" />
            <Property PropertyID="SMBIOSMinorVersion" />
            <Property PropertyID="SMBIOSPresent" />
            <Property PropertyID="SoftwareElementID" />
            <Property PropertyID="SoftwareElementState" />
            <Property PropertyID="Status" />
            <Property PropertyID="TargetOperatingSystem" />
            <Property PropertyID="Version" />
          </DiscoveryClass>
        </DiscoveryTypes>
        <DataSource ID="DS"
TypeID="Windows!Microsoft.Windows.TimedScript.DiscoveryProvider"><IntervalSe
conds>8640</IntervalSeconds><SyncTime
/><ScriptName>Win32_BIOS.js</ScriptName><Arguments>$MPElement$
$Target/Id$
$Target/Property[Type="Windows!Microsoft.Windows.Computer"]/PrincipalName$
</Arguments><ScriptBody>
                var oArgs = WScript.Arguments;
                if (oArgs.length != 3)
                {
                   WScript.Quit(-1);
                }
                var SourceID = oArgs(0);
                var ManagedEntityId = oArgs(1);
                var TargetComputer = oArgs(2);
                var oAPI = new ActiveXObject("MOM.ScriptAPI");
                var oDiscoveryData = oAPI.CreateDiscoveryData(0, SourceID,
ManagedEntityId);
                var oInst =
oDiscoveryData.CreateClassInstance("$MPElement[Name='PlanetMPs.Win32_BIOS.
Class']$");
```

```
oInst.AddProperty("$MPElement[Name='Windows!Microsoft.Windows.Computer']/P
rincipalName$", TargetComputer);
                var l = new ActiveXObject("WbemScripting.SWbemLocator");
                var svc = l.ConnectServer(TargetComputer, "root\\CIMV2");
                var objs = svc.InstancesOf("Win32_BIOS");
                var enumItems = new Enumerator(objs);
                for (; !enumItems.atEnd(); enumItems.moveNext())
                {
                    var obj = enumItems.item();

oInst.AddProperty("$MPElement[Name='PlanetMPs.Win32_BIOS.Class']/BiosCharac
teristics$", GetValue("BiosCharacteristics", obj));

oInst.AddProperty("$MPElement[Name='PlanetMPs.Win32_BIOS.Class']/BIOSVersio
n$", GetValue("BIOSVersion", obj));

oInst.AddProperty("$MPElement[Name='PlanetMPs.Win32_BIOS.Class']/BuildNumb
er$", GetValue("BuildNumber", obj));

oInst.AddProperty("$MPElement[Name='PlanetMPs.Win32_BIOS.Class']/Caption$",
GetValue("Caption", obj));

oInst.AddProperty("$MPElement[Name='PlanetMPs.Win32_BIOS.Class']/CodeSet$",
GetValue("CodeSet", obj));

oInst.AddProperty("$MPElement[Name='PlanetMPs.Win32_BIOS.Class']/CurrentLa
nguage$", GetValue("CurrentLanguage", obj));

oInst.AddProperty("$MPElement[Name='PlanetMPs.Win32_BIOS.Class']/Descriptio
n$", GetValue("Description", obj));

oInst.AddProperty("$MPElement[Name='PlanetMPs.Win32_BIOS.Class']/Identificati
onCode$", GetValue("IdentificationCode", obj));

oInst.AddProperty("$MPElement[Name='PlanetMPs.Win32_BIOS.Class']/Installable
Languages$", GetValue("InstallableLanguages", obj));

oInst.AddProperty("$MPElement[Name='PlanetMPs.Win32_BIOS.Class']/InstallDate
$", GetValue("InstallDate", obj));
```

```
oInst.AddProperty("$MPElement[Name='PlanetMPs.Win32_BIOS.Class']/LanguageE
dition$", GetValue("LanguageEdition", obj));

oInst.AddProperty("$MPElement[Name='PlanetMPs.Win32_BIOS.Class']/ListOfLang
uages$", GetValue("ListOfLanguages", obj));

oInst.AddProperty("$MPElement[Name='PlanetMPs.Win32_BIOS.Class']/Manufactu
rer$", GetValue("Manufacturer", obj));

oInst.AddProperty("$MPElement[Name='PlanetMPs.Win32_BIOS.Class']/Name$",
GetValue("Name", obj));

oInst.AddProperty("$MPElement[Name='PlanetMPs.Win32_BIOS.Class']/OtherTarge
tOS$", GetValue("OtherTargetOS", obj));

oInst.AddProperty("$MPElement[Name='PlanetMPs.Win32_BIOS.Class']/PrimaryBI
OS$", GetValue("PrimaryBIOS", obj));

oInst.AddProperty("$MPElement[Name='PlanetMPs.Win32_BIOS.Class']/ReleaseDat
e$", GetValue("ReleaseDate", obj));

oInst.AddProperty("$MPElement[Name='PlanetMPs.Win32_BIOS.Class']/SerialNum
ber$", GetValue("SerialNumber", obj));

oInst.AddProperty("$MPElement[Name='PlanetMPs.Win32_BIOS.Class']/SMBIOSBI
OSVersion$", GetValue("SMBIOSBIOSVersion", obj));

oInst.AddProperty("$MPElement[Name='PlanetMPs.Win32_BIOS.Class']/SMBIOSMa
jorVersion$", GetValue("SMBIOSMajorVersion", obj));

oInst.AddProperty("$MPElement[Name='PlanetMPs.Win32_BIOS.Class']/SMBIOSMi
norVersion$", GetValue("SMBIOSMinorVersion", obj));

oInst.AddProperty("$MPElement[Name='PlanetMPs.Win32_BIOS.Class']/SMBIOSPre
sent$", GetValue("SMBIOSPresent", obj));

oInst.AddProperty("$MPElement[Name='PlanetMPs.Win32_BIOS.Class']/SoftwareEl
ementID$", GetValue("SoftwareElementID", obj));
```

```
oInst.AddProperty("$MPElement[Name='PlanetMPs.Win32_BIOS.Class']/SoftwareEl
ementState$", GetValue("SoftwareElementState", obj));

oInst.AddProperty("$MPElement[Name='PlanetMPs.Win32_BIOS.Class']/Status$",
GetValue("Status", obj));

oInst.AddProperty("$MPElement[Name='PlanetMPs.Win32_BIOS.Class']/TargetOper
atingSystem$", GetValue("TargetOperatingSystem", obj));

oInst.AddProperty("$MPElement[Name='PlanetMPs.Win32_BIOS.Class']/Version$",
GetValue("Version", obj));
                    break;
            }
            oDiscoveryData.AddInstance(oInst);
            oAPI.Return(oDiscoveryData);
            function GetValue(Name, obj)
            {
                var tempstr = new String();
                var tempstr1 = new String();
                var tName = new String();
                tempstr1 = obj.GetObjectText_();
                var re = /"/g;
                tempstr1 = tempstr1.replace(re , "");
                var pos;
                tName = Name + " = ";
                pos = tempstr1.indexOf(tName);
                if (pos &gt; -1)
                {
                  pos = pos + tName.length;
                  tempstr = tempstr1.substring(pos, tempstr1.length);
                  pos = tempstr.indexOf(";");
                  tempstr = tempstr.substring(0, pos);
                  tempstr = tempstr.replace("{", "");
                  tempstr = tempstr.replace("}", "");
                  if (tempstr.length &gt; 13)
                  {
                    if (obj.Properties_(Name).CIMType == 101)
                    {
```

```
                    tempstr = tempstr.substr(4, 2) + "/"  + tempstr.substr(6, 2) +
"/" + tempstr.substr(0, 3) + " " + tempstr.substr(8, 2) + ":" + tempstr.substr(10, 2) +
":" + tempstr.substr(12, 2);
                    }
                }
                return tempstr;
            }
            else
            {
                return "";
            }
        }
```

```xml
</ScriptBody><TimeoutSeconds>120</TimeoutSeconds></DataSource>
        </Discovery>
      </Discoveries>
    </Monitoring>
    <Presentation>
      <Views>
        <View ID="PlanetMPs.Win32__BIOS.Class.Discovery.StateView"
Accessibility="Internal" Enabled="true" Target="PlanetMPs.Win32__BIOS.Class"
TypeID="SC!Microsoft.SystemCenter.StateViewType" Visible="true">
          <Category>Operations</Category><Criteria /></View>
      </Views>
      <Folders>
        <Folder ID="PlanetMPs.Win32__BIOS.ManagementPack.ViewFolder.Root"
Accessibility="Internal"
ParentFolder="SC!Microsoft.SystemCenter.Monitoring.ViewFolder.Root" />
      </Folders>
      <FolderItems>
        <FolderItem ElementID="PlanetMPs.Win32__BIOS.Class.Discovery.StateView"
Folder="PlanetMPs.Win32__BIOS.ManagementPack.ViewFolder.Root" />
      </FolderItems>
    </Presentation>
    <LanguagePacks>
      <LanguagePack ID="ENU" IsDefault="true">
        <DisplayStrings>
          <DisplayString ElementID="PlanetMPs.Win32__BIOS.ManagementPack">
            <Name>PlanetMPs Win32__BIOS ManagementPack</Name>
```

```xml
      <Description>Discovers Win32_BIOS</Description>
    </DisplayString>
    <DisplayString ElementID="PlanetMPs.Win32_BIOS.Class">
      <Name>PlanetMPs Win32_BIOS</Name>
      <Description>Creates A SQL table for PlanetMPs Win32_BIOS where
discovery information will be stored.</Description>
    </DisplayString>
    <DisplayString ElementID="PlanetMPs.Win32_BIOS.Class.Discovery">
      <Name>PlanetMPs Win32_BIOS  Class Discovery</Name>
      <Description>Discovers and populates the SQL table for PlanetMPs
Win32_BIOS</Description>
    </DisplayString>
    <DisplayString ElementID="PlanetMPs.Win32_BIOS.Class"
SubElementID="BiosCharacteristics">
      <Name>BiosCharacteristics</Name>
    </DisplayString>
    <DisplayString ElementID="PlanetMPs.Win32_BIOS.Class"
SubElementID="BIOSVersion">
      <Name>BIOSVersion</Name>
    </DisplayString>
    <DisplayString ElementID="PlanetMPs.Win32_BIOS.Class"
SubElementID="BuildNumber">
      <Name>BuildNumber</Name>
    </DisplayString>
    <DisplayString ElementID="PlanetMPs.Win32_BIOS.Class"
SubElementID="Caption">
      <Name>Caption</Name>
    </DisplayString>
    <DisplayString ElementID="PlanetMPs.Win32_BIOS.Class"
SubElementID="CodeSet">
      <Name>CodeSet</Name>
    </DisplayString>
    <DisplayString ElementID="PlanetMPs.Win32_BIOS.Class"
SubElementID="CurrentLanguage">
      <Name>CurrentLanguage</Name>
    </DisplayString>
    <DisplayString ElementID="PlanetMPs.Win32_BIOS.Class"
SubElementID="Description">
      <Name>Description</Name>
    </DisplayString>
```

```xml
<DisplayString ElementID="PlanetMPs.Win32_BIOS.Class"
SubElementID="IdentificationCode">
       <Name>IdentificationCode</Name>
       </DisplayString>
       <DisplayString ElementID="PlanetMPs.Win32_BIOS.Class"
SubElementID="InstallableLanguages">
        <Name>InstallableLanguages</Name>
       </DisplayString>
       <DisplayString ElementID="PlanetMPs.Win32_BIOS.Class"
SubElementID="InstallDate">
        <Name>InstallDate</Name>
       </DisplayString>
       <DisplayString ElementID="PlanetMPs.Win32_BIOS.Class"
SubElementID="LanguageEdition">
        <Name>LanguageEdition</Name>
       </DisplayString>
       <DisplayString ElementID="PlanetMPs.Win32_BIOS.Class"
SubElementID="ListOfLanguages">
        <Name>ListOfLanguages</Name>
       </DisplayString>
       <DisplayString ElementID="PlanetMPs.Win32_BIOS.Class"
SubElementID="Manufacturer">
        <Name>Manufacturer</Name>
       </DisplayString>
       <DisplayString ElementID="PlanetMPs.Win32_BIOS.Class"
SubElementID="Name">
        <Name>Name</Name>
       </DisplayString>
       <DisplayString ElementID="PlanetMPs.Win32_BIOS.Class"
SubElementID="OtherTargetOS">
        <Name>OtherTargetOS</Name>
       </DisplayString>
       <DisplayString ElementID="PlanetMPs.Win32_BIOS.Class"
SubElementID="PrimaryBIOS">
        <Name>PrimaryBIOS</Name>
       </DisplayString>
       <DisplayString ElementID="PlanetMPs.Win32_BIOS.Class"
SubElementID="ReleaseDate">
        <Name>ReleaseDate</Name>
       </DisplayString>
```

```xml
<DisplayString ElementID="PlanetMPs.Win32_BIOS.Class"
SubElementID="SerialNumber">
     <Name>SerialNumber</Name>
     </DisplayString>
     <DisplayString ElementID="PlanetMPs.Win32_BIOS.Class"
SubElementID="SMBIOSBIOSVersion">
     <Name>SMBIOSBIOSVersion</Name>
     </DisplayString>
     <DisplayString ElementID="PlanetMPs.Win32_BIOS.Class"
SubElementID="SMBIOSMajorVersion">
     <Name>SMBIOSMajorVersion</Name>
     </DisplayString>
     <DisplayString ElementID="PlanetMPs.Win32_BIOS.Class"
SubElementID="SMBIOSMinorVersion">
     <Name>SMBIOSMinorVersion</Name>
     </DisplayString>
     <DisplayString ElementID="PlanetMPs.Win32_BIOS.Class"
SubElementID="SMBIOSPresent">
     <Name>SMBIOSPresent</Name>
     </DisplayString>
     <DisplayString ElementID="PlanetMPs.Win32_BIOS.Class"
SubElementID="SoftwareElementID">
     <Name>SoftwareElementID</Name>
     </DisplayString>
     <DisplayString ElementID="PlanetMPs.Win32_BIOS.Class"
SubElementID="SoftwareElementState">
     <Name>SoftwareElementState</Name>
     </DisplayString>
     <DisplayString ElementID="PlanetMPs.Win32_BIOS.Class"
SubElementID="Status">
     <Name>Status</Name>
     </DisplayString>
     <DisplayString ElementID="PlanetMPs.Win32_BIOS.Class"
SubElementID="TargetOperatingSystem">
     <Name>TargetOperatingSystem</Name>
     </DisplayString>
     <DisplayString ElementID="PlanetMPs.Win32_BIOS.Class"
SubElementID="Version">
     <Name>Version</Name>
     </DisplayString>
```

```xml
    <DisplayString
ElementID="PlanetMPs.Win32_BIOS.Class.Discovery.StateView">
      <Name>State</Name>
      <Description>Discovers and displays information for
Win32_BIOS</Description>
      </DisplayString>
      <DisplayString
ElementID="PlanetMPs.Win32_BIOS.ManagementPack.ViewFolder.Root">
      <Name>PlanetMPs Win32_BIOS</Name>
      </DisplayString>
     </DisplayStrings>
    </LanguagePack>
   </LanguagePacks>
   </ManagementPack>
```

In fact, what if you could create a program that not only creates the MP in less than a minute, imports it into SCOM, waits for all the machines it is supposed to run on within a reasonable amount of time, then creates an SRS report and deletes the MP?

Before we build this, you need to know what an MP is and then see how these pieces work together.

The crude but bare Bones Management Pack

It may not do anything bit it imports

An acquittance of mine who was the Program Manager For SCOM 2007 told me not to learn how to read the XML. Said it would drive me crazy.

I didn't listen to him.

Take a look at the bare bones version of an MP in its XML format:

```xml
<ManagementPack ContentReadable="true" xmlns:xsd="http://www.w3.org/2001/XMLSchema"
xmlns:xsl="http://www.w3.org/1999/XSL/Transform">
  <Manifest>
   <Identity>
    <ID>PlanetMPs</ID>
    <Version>1.0.0.0</Version>
   </Identity>
   <Name>PlanetMPs</Name>
   <References>
    <Reference Alias="SC">
     <ID>Microsoft.SystemCenter.Library</ID>
     <Version>6.1.7221.0</Version>
     <PublicKeyToken>31bf3856ad364e35</PublicKeyToken>
    </Reference>
    <Reference Alias="Windows">
     <ID>Microsoft.Windows.Library</ID>
     <Version>6.1.7221.0</Version>
     <PublicKeyToken>31bf3856ad364e35</PublicKeyToken>
    </Reference>
    <Reference Alias="Health">
     <ID>System.Health.Library</ID>
     <Version>6.1.7221.0</Version>
     <PublicKeyToken>31bf3856ad364e35</PublicKeyToken>
    </Reference>
    <Reference Alias="System">
```

```
      <ID>System.Library</ID>
      <Version>6.1.7221.0</Version>
      <PublicKeyToken>31bf3856ad364e35</PublicKeyToken>
     </Reference>
    </References>
   </Manifest>
   <LanguagePacks>
    <LanguagePack ID="ENU" IsDefault="true">
     <DisplayStrings>
      <DisplayString ElementID="PlanetMPs">
       <Name>PlanetMPs</Name>
      </DisplayString>
     </DisplayStrings>
    </LanguagePack>
   </LanguagePacks>
 </ManagementPack>
```

This is from the SCOM 2007 R2 Authoring console and can easily be reproduced in code. But before we do, let's beak this down into something that makes sense.

```
<ManagementPack ContentReadable="true" xmlns:xsd="http://www.w3.org/2001/XMLSchema"
xmlns:xsl="http://www.w3.org/1999/XSL/Transform">
    <Manifest>
     <Identity>
      <ID>PlanetMPs</ID>
      <Version>1.0.0.0</Version>
     </Identity>
     <Name>PlanetMPs</Name>
```

There are a lot of very important things going on here. For example, the very first line – the stuff between <ManagementPack > - tells us that you can read the content, there is a xsl definition table and there is a xslt or transformation template at work that works with the xml so that it can be filtered and made sense of the all the xml tags that follow. At this point, we don't need to know how it works just that it does.

Next we have the Manifest tag which will have its end tag at the end of the references. The next two tags <Identity> and <Name> are, perhaps, the most important tags in the ManagementPack.

There are two tags between the <Identity></Identity> which are of the utmost importance. The ID of the MP must exactly match the filename – the .xml extension.

If you make changes to the file, the version must be changed otherwise when the modified file will be seen by SCOM as the same file that was imported and no response to the changes will occur. If the version is 1.0.0.0 then the number would be 1.0.0.1 when it gets imported.

Many of us have found it to be much easier to take the ID and put spaces where the dots were. For example, PlanetMPs.Win32_Bios.Discovery.ManagementPack would become PlanetMPs Win32_Bios Discovery ManagementPack.

REFERENCES

If you are programmer familiar with the concept of making a reference to a namespace, you know that in doing so, you're now able to use the functionality available by using the objects, setting properties and working interactively with methods.

Well, references kind of work the same way inside a Management Pack. I say kind of because the references don't really help you with code complete. In fact, they don't help you at all. Tons of opportunities, hundreds or possibilities and none are all documented anywhere.

This was my complaint back in 2007, it is still a major flaw in the product. And where would you start, if you could? Turns out, the System.Library is where you would start. If you were to convert that file, below is the code:

```vb
Imports Microsoft.EnterpriseManagement.Configuration
Imports Microsoft.EnterpriseManagement.Configuration.IO

Public Class Form1

    Private Sub OpenToolStripMenuItem_Click(sender As System.Object, e As System.EventArgs) Handles OpenToolStripMenuItem.Click
        Dim OpenFileDialog As New OpenFileDialog
        OpenFileDialog.InitialDirectory = My.Computer.FileSystem.SpecialDirectories.MyDocuments
        OpenFileDialog.Filter = "Text Files (*.mp)|*.mp"
        If (OpenFileDialog.ShowDialog(Me) = System.Windows.Forms.DialogResult.OK) Then
            Dim FileName As String = OpenFileDialog.FileName
            Dim mp As New ManagementPack(Filename)
            Dim xmlWriter As New ManagementPackXmlWriter(Application.StartupPath)
            Dim xmlFile As String = xmlWriter.WriteManagementPack(mp)
            WebBrowser1.Navigate(xmlFile)

        End If
```

End Sub

Private Sub **Form1_Load**(sender As **System**.Object, e As **System**.EventArgs) Handles MyBase.**Load**

End Sub
End Class

Just go over to the ManagementPack folder you used to install SCOM from and look for System.Library.mp.

Also, to make the above code work, The form might look like this:

```
File

- <ManagementPack ContentReadable="true" xmlns:xsd="http://www.w3.org/2001/XMLSchema"
  xmlns:xsl="http://www.w3.org/1999/XSL/Transform">
  - <Manifest>
    - <Identity>
        <ID>Microsoft.SystemCenter.Library</ID>
        <Version>6.1.7221.0</Version>
      </Identity>
      <Name>Microsoft System Center Library</Name>
    - <References>
      - <Reference Alias="Windows">
          <ID>Microsoft.Windows.Library</ID>
          <Version>6.1.7221.0</Version>
          <PublicKeyToken>31bf3856ad364e35</PublicKeyToken>
        </Reference>
      - <Reference Alias="AppLog">
          <ID>System.ApplicationLog.Library</ID>
          <Version>6.1.7221.0</Version>
          <PublicKeyToken>31bf3856ad364e35</PublicKeyToken>
        </Reference>
      - <Reference Alias="Health">
          <ID>System.Health.Library</ID>
          <Version>6.1.7221.0</Version>
          <PublicKeyToken>31bf3856ad364e35</PublicKeyToken>
        </Reference>
      - <Reference Alias="System">
          <ID>System.Library</ID>
          <Version>6.1.7221.0</Version>
          <PublicKeyToken>31bf3856ad364e35</PublicKeyToken>
        </Reference>
      - <Reference Alias="Performance">
          <ID>System.Performance.Library</ID>
          <Version>6.1.7221.0</Version>
          <PublicKeyToken>31bf3856ad364e35</PublicKeyToken>
        </Reference>
      - <Reference Alias="Snmp">
          <ID>System.Snmp.Library</ID>
          <Version>6.1.7221.0</Version>
          <PublicKeyToken>31bf3856ad364e35</PublicKeyToken>
        </Reference>
      </References>
    </Manifest>
```

Above is the System.Library. Here's the beginning of the
Microsoft.SystemCenter.Library:

```
File

- <ManagementPack ContentReadable="true" xmlns:xsd="http://www.w3.org/2001/XMLSchema"
    xmlns:xsl="http://www.w3.org/1999/XSL/Transform">
  - <Manifest>
    - <Identity>
        <ID>Microsoft.SystemCenter.Library</ID>
        <Version>6.1.7221.0</Version>
      </Identity>
      <Name>Microsoft System Center Library</Name>
    - <References>
      - <Reference Alias="Windows">
          <ID>Microsoft.Windows.Library</ID>
          <Version>6.1.7221.0</Version>
          <PublicKeyToken>31bf3856ad364e35</PublicKeyToken>
        </Reference>
      - <Reference Alias="AppLog">
          <ID>System.ApplicationLog.Library</ID>
          <Version>6.1.7221.0</Version>
          <PublicKeyToken>31bf3856ad364e35</PublicKeyToken>
        </Reference>
      - <Reference Alias="Health">
          <ID>System.Health.Library</ID>
          <Version>6.1.7221.0</Version>
          <PublicKeyToken>31bf3856ad364e35</PublicKeyToken>
        </Reference>
      - <Reference Alias="System">
          <ID>System.Library</ID>
          <Version>6.1.7221.0</Version>
          <PublicKeyToken>31bf3856ad364e35</PublicKeyToken>
        </Reference>
      - <Reference Alias="Performance">
          <ID>System.Performance.Library</ID>
          <Version>6.1.7221.0</Version>
          <PublicKeyToken>31bf3856ad364e35</PublicKeyToken>
        </Reference>
      - <Reference Alias="Snmp">
          <ID>System.Snmp.Library</ID>
          <Version>6.1.7221.0</Version>
          <PublicKeyToken>31bf3856ad364e35</PublicKeyToken>
        </Reference>
      </References>
    </Manifest>
```

Here's the Microsoft.Windows.Library:

```
- <ManagementPack
    xsi:noNamespaceSchemaLocation="..\..\..\sdk\server\MPInfrastructure\schema\ManagementPackSch
    xmlns:xsd="http://www.w3.org/2001/XMLSchema"
    xmlns:xsi="http://www.w3.org/2001/XMLSchema-instance">
  - <Manifest>
    - <Identity>
        <ID>Microsoft.Windows.Library</ID>
        <Version>6.1.7221.0</Version>
      </Identity>
      <Name>Microsoft Windows Library</Name>
    - <References>
      - <Reference Alias="Health">
          <ID>System.Health.Library</ID>
          <Version>6.1.7221.0</Version>
          <PublicKeyToken>31bf3856ad364e35</PublicKeyToken>
        </Reference>
      - <Reference Alias="System">
          <ID>System.Library</ID>
          <Version>6.1.7221.0</Version>
          <PublicKeyToken>31bf3856ad364e35</PublicKeyToken>
        </Reference>
      - <Reference Alias="Performance">
          <ID>System.Performance.Library</ID>
          <Version>6.1.7221.0</Version>
          <PublicKeyToken>31bf3856ad364e35</PublicKeyToken>
        </Reference>
      </References>
    </Manifest>
```

And, last but not least is the System.Health.Library:

```
- <ManagementPack
    xsi:noNamespaceSchemaLocation="..\..\..\sdk\server\MPInfrastructure\schema\ManagementPack:
    xmlns:xsd="http://www.w3.org/2001/XMLSchema"
    xmlns:xsi="http://www.w3.org/2001/XMLSchema-instance">
  - <Manifest>
    - <Identity>
        <ID>System.Health.Library</ID>
        <Version>6.1.7221.0</Version>
      </Identity>
      <Name>System Health Library</Name>
    - <References>
      - <Reference Alias="System">
          <ID>System.Library</ID>
          <Version>6.1.7221.0</Version>
          <PublicKeyToken>31bf3856ad364e35</PublicKeyToken>
        </Reference>
      </References>
    </Manifest>
```

And the one that was added to the Management Pack that was created by the automation. The System.Performance.Libraray:

```
- <ManagementPack
    xsi:noNamespaceSchemaLocation="..\..\..\sdk\server\MPInfrastructure\schema\ManagementPackSche
    xmlns:xsd="http://www.w3.org/2001/XMLSchema"
    xmlns:xsi="http://www.w3.org/2001/XMLSchema-instance">
  - <Manifest>
    - <Identity>
        <ID>System.Performance.Library</ID>
        <Version>6.1.7221.0</Version>
      </Identity>
      <Name>System Performance Library</Name>
    - <References>
      - <Reference Alias="Health">
          <ID>System.Health.Library</ID>
          <Version>6.1.7221.0</Version>
          <PublicKeyToken>31bf3856ad364e35</PublicKeyToken>
        </Reference>
      - <Reference Alias="System">
          <ID>System.Library</ID>
          <Version>6.1.7221.0</Version>
          <PublicKeyToken>31bf3856ad364e35</PublicKeyToken>
        </Reference>
      - <Reference Alias="Snmp">
          <ID>System.Snmp.Library</ID>
          <Version>6.1.7221.0</Version>
          <PublicKeyToken>31bf3856ad364e35</PublicKeyToken>
        </Reference>
      </References>
    </Manifest>
```

I purposely left out all the nuts and bolts so to speak because it would have taken thousands of pages to do so. It is better, right now, to stay focused on the Management Pack we are creating through automation.

Classes

Classes and discovers are, essentially, the building blocks of a Management Pack. Classes build tables in SQL Server and Discoveries populate them.

```
<ClassType ID="PlanetMPs.Win32_BIOS.Class" Accessibility="Internal"
Abstract="false" Base="Windows!Microsoft.Windows.LocalApplication"
Hosted="true" Singleton="false">
        <Property ID="BiosCharacteristics" Type="string" Key="false" />
        <Property ID="BIOSVersion" Type="string" Key="false" />
        <Property ID="BuildNumber" Type="string" Key="false" />
        <Property ID="Caption" Type="string" Key="false" />
        <Property ID="CodeSet" Type="string" Key="false" />
        <Property ID="CurrentLanguage" Type="string" Key="false" />
        <Property ID="Description" Type="string" Key="false" />
        <Property ID="IdentificationCode" Type="string" Key="false" />
        <Property ID="InstallableLanguages" Type="string" Key="false" />
```

```
    <Property ID="InstallDate" Type="string" Key="false" />
    <Property ID="LanguageEdition" Type="string" Key="false" />
    <Property ID="ListOfLanguages" Type="string" Key="false" />
    <Property ID="Manufacturer" Type="string" Key="false" />
    <Property ID="Name" Type="string" Key="false" />
    <Property ID="OtherTargetOS" Type="string" Key="false" />
    <Property ID="PrimaryBIOS" Type="string" Key="false" />
    <Property ID="ReleaseDate" Type="string" Key="false" />
    <Property ID="SerialNumber" Type="string" Key="false" />
    <Property ID="SMBIOSBIOSVersion" Type="string" Key="false" />
    <Property ID="SMBIOSMajorVersion" Type="string" Key="false" />
    <Property ID="SMBIOSMinorVersion" Type="string" Key="false" />
    <Property ID="SMBIOSPresent" Type="string" Key="false" />
    <Property ID="SoftwareElementID" Type="string" Key="false" />
    <Property ID="SoftwareElementState" Type="string" Key="false" />
    <Property ID="Status" Type="string" Key="false" />
    <Property ID="TargetOperatingSystem" Type="string" Key="false" />
    <Property ID="Version" Type="string" Key="false" />
</ClassType>
```

There three of things we need to discuss here. First, this:

```
Base="Windows!Microsoft.Windows.LocalApplication"
```

When this reference was made:

```
<Reference Alias="Windows">
    <ID>Microsoft.Windows.Library</ID>
    <Version>6.0.4941.0</Version>
    <PublicKeyToken>31bf3856ad364e35</PublicKeyToken>
    </Reference>
```

Inside that library is:

```
<ClassType ID="Microsoft.Windows.LocalApplication"
Base="System!System.LocalApplication" Accessibility="Public" Hosted="true"
Abstract="true" />
```

To use it, once the reference is made, to bind to it, the Alias for the library is used followed by the exclamation sign and then the name of the class that gets reference.

Two, the property node and the Key attribute. You can only use one that you set to true. You do this when you know that there is more than one row you want recorded by the Discovery. Otherwise, they are all set to false.

The third point: You are in the driver's seat when it comes to what you want discovered and recorded in your database. The more information you glean from other machines the longer it takes to collect the information. Administrators call that "noise".

The Discovery

There are a wide variety of discovery DataSource types that can be used. In this particular case, we're using the:

Windows!Microsoft.Windows.TimedScript.DiscoveryProvider.

This works with VBScript, Perlscript and Jscript. The one that works with PowerShell is:

Windows!Microsoft.Windows.TimedPowerShell.DiscoveryProvider

Below is what this looks like:

```
<DataSourceModuleType ID="Microsoft.Windows.TimedScript.DiscoveryProvider" Accessibility="Public">
  <Configuration>
    <IncludeSchemaTypes>
    <SchemaType>System!System.ExpressionEvaluatorSchema</SchemaType>
     <SchemaType>System!System.CommandExecuterSchema</SchemaType>
    </IncludeSchemaTypes>
    <xsd:element name="IntervalSeconds" type="xsd:int" />
    <xsd:element name="SyncTime" type="xsd:string" />
    <xsd:element name="ScriptName" type="xsd:string" />
    <xsd:element name="Arguments" type="xsd:string" />
    <xsd:element name="ScriptBody" type="xsd:string" />
    <xsd:element name="SecureInput" minOccurs="0" maxOccurs="1">
     <xsd:simpleType>
      <xsd:restriction base="xsd:string">
       <xsd:maxLength value="256" />
      </xsd:restriction>
     </xsd:simpleType>
    </xsd:element>
    <xsd:element name="TimeoutSeconds" type="xsd:integer" />
    <xsd:element minOccurs="0" maxOccurs="1" name="EventPolicy"
type="CommandExecuterEventPolicyType" />
  </Configuration>
  <OverrideableParameters>
```

```xml
        <OverrideableParameter ID="IntervalSeconds" Selector="$Config/IntervalSeconds$"
ParameterType="int" />
        <OverrideableParameter ID="SyncTime" Selector="$Config/SyncTime$" ParameterType="string" />
        <OverrideableParameter ID="Arguments" Selector="$Config/Arguments$" ParameterType="string"
/>
        <OverrideableParameter ID="TimeoutSeconds" Selector="$Config/TimeoutSeconds$"
ParameterType="int" />
      </OverrideableParameters>
      <ModuleImplementation>
        <Composite>
          <MemberModules>
            <DataSource TypeID="System!System.Discovery.Scheduler" ID="DS1">
              <Scheduler>
                <SimpleReccuringSchedule>
                  <Interval>$Config/IntervalSeconds$</Interval>
                  <SyncTime>$Config/SyncTime$</SyncTime>
                </SimpleReccuringSchedule>
                <ExcludeDates />
              </Scheduler>
            </DataSource>
            <ProbeAction TypeID="Microsoft.Windows.ScriptDiscoveryProbe" ID="Script">
              <ScriptName>$Config/ScriptName$</ScriptName>
              <Arguments>$Config/Arguments$</Arguments>
              <ScriptBody>$Config/ScriptBody$</ScriptBody>
              <SecureInput>$Config/SecureInput$</SecureInput>
              <TimeoutSeconds>$Config/TimeoutSeconds$</TimeoutSeconds>
              <EventPolicy>$Config/EventPolicy$</EventPolicy>
            </ProbeAction>
          </MemberModules>
          <Composition>
            <Node ID="Script">
              <Node ID="DS1" />
            </Node>
          </Composition>
        </Composite>
      </ModuleImplementation>
      <OutputType>System!System.Discovery.Data</OutputType>
    </DataSourceModuleType>
```

This particular Module Type provider is a composite module meaning it is a
collection of activities:

It uses a DataSource Module Type:

```xml
<DataSource TypeID="System!System.Discovery.Scheduler" ID="DS1">
```

And it uses a ProbeAction Module Type:

```xml
<ProbeAction TypeID="Microsoft.Windows.ScriptDiscoveryProbe" ID="Script">
```

Furthermore, you pass in the following:

```
<xsd:element name="IntervalSeconds" type="xsd:int" />
<xsd:element name="SyncTime" type="xsd:string" />
<xsd:element name="ScriptName" type="xsd:string" />
<xsd:element name="Arguments" type="xsd:string" />
<xsd:element name="ScriptBody" type="xsd:string" />
```

But initially, you add the class information to it as seen below:

```
<Discovery ID="PlanetMPs.Win32_BIOS.Class.Discovery" Enabled="true"
Target="Windows!Microsoft.Windows.Computer" ConfirmDelivery="false"
Remotable="true" Priority="Normal">
    <Category>Discovery</Category>
    <DiscoveryTypes>
     <DiscoveryClass TypeID="PlanetMPs.Win32_BIOS.Class">
      <Property PropertyID="BiosCharacteristics" />
      <Property PropertyID="BIOSVersion" />
      <Property PropertyID="BuildNumber" />
      <Property PropertyID="Caption" />
      <Property PropertyID="CodeSet" />
      <Property PropertyID="CurrentLanguage" />
      <Property PropertyID="Description" />
      <Property PropertyID="IdentificationCode" />
      <Property PropertyID="InstallableLanguages" />
      <Property PropertyID="InstallDate" />
      <Property PropertyID="LanguageEdition" />
      <Property PropertyID="ListOfLanguages" />
      <Property PropertyID="Manufacturer" />
      <Property PropertyID="Name" />
      <Property PropertyID="OtherTargetOS" />
      <Property PropertyID="PrimaryBIOS" />
      <Property PropertyID="ReleaseDate" />
      <Property PropertyID="SerialNumber" />
      <Property PropertyID="SMBIOSBIOSVersion" />
      <Property PropertyID="SMBIOSMajorVersion" />
      <Property PropertyID="SMBIOSMinorVersion" />
      <Property PropertyID="SMBIOSPresent" />
      <Property PropertyID="SoftwareElementID" />
      <Property PropertyID="SoftwareElementState" />
      <Property PropertyID="Status" />
```

```
    <Property PropertyID="TargetOperatingSystem" />
    <Property PropertyID="Version" />
  </DiscoveryClass>
</DiscoveryTypes>
```

Then, you reference the DataSource:

```
<DataSource ID="DS"
TypeID="Windows!Microsoft.Windows.TimedScript.DiscoveryProvider">
```

Once we have made the connection to the Data Source, we set the values it expects so that it works:

```
<xsd:element name="IntervalSeconds" type="xsd:int" />
<xsd:element name="SyncTime" type="xsd:string" />
<xsd:element name="ScriptName" type="xsd:string" />
<xsd:element name="Arguments" type="xsd:string" />
<xsd:element name="ScriptBody" type="xsd:string" />
```

```
<IntervalSeconds>8640</IntervalSeconds>
<SyncTime/>
<ScriptName>Win32_BIOS.js</ScriptName>
<Arguments>$MPElement$ $Target/Id$
$Target/Property[Type="Windows!Microsoft.Windows.Computer"]/PrincipalName$
</Arguments>
<ScriptBody>
```

At this point we add the script:

```
var oArgs = WScript.Arguments;
if (oArgs.length != 3)
{
  WScript.Quit(-1);
}
var SourceID = oArgs(0);
var ManagedEntityId = oArgs(1);
var TargetComputer = oArgs(2);
var oAPI = new ActiveXObject("MOM.ScriptAPI");
```

```
          var oDiscoveryData = oAPI.CreateDiscoveryData(0, SourceID,
ManagedEntityId);
          var oInst =
oDiscoveryData.CreateClassInstance("$MPElement[Name='PlanetMPs.Win32_BIOS.
Class']$");

oInst.AddProperty("$MPElement[Name='Windows!Microsoft.Windows.Computer']/P
rincipalName$", TargetComputer);
          var l = new ActiveXObject("WbemScripting.SWbemLocator");
          var svc = l.ConnectServer(TargetComputer, "root\\CIMV2");
          var objs = svc.InstancesOf("Win32_BIOS");
          var enumItems = new Enumerator(objs);
          for (; !enumItems.atEnd(); enumItems.moveNext())
          {
            var obj = enumItems.item();

oInst.AddProperty("$MPElement[Name='PlanetMPs.Win32_BIOS.Class']/BiosCharac
teristics$", GetValue("BiosCharacteristics", obj));

oInst.AddProperty("$MPElement[Name='PlanetMPs.Win32_BIOS.Class']/BIOSVersio
n$", GetValue("BIOSVersion", obj));

oInst.AddProperty("$MPElement[Name='PlanetMPs.Win32_BIOS.Class']/BuildNumb
er$", GetValue("BuildNumber", obj));

oInst.AddProperty("$MPElement[Name='PlanetMPs.Win32_BIOS.Class']/Caption$",
GetValue("Caption", obj));

oInst.AddProperty("$MPElement[Name='PlanetMPs.Win32_BIOS.Class']/CodeSet$",
GetValue("CodeSet", obj));

oInst.AddProperty("$MPElement[Name='PlanetMPs.Win32_BIOS.Class']/CurrentLa
nguage$", GetValue("CurrentLanguage", obj));

oInst.AddProperty("$MPElement[Name='PlanetMPs.Win32_BIOS.Class']/Descriptio
n$", GetValue("Description", obj));

oInst.AddProperty("$MPElement[Name='PlanetMPs.Win32_BIOS.Class']/Identificati
onCode$", GetValue("IdentificationCode", obj));
```

```
oInst.AddProperty("$MPElement[Name='PlanetMPs.Win32_BIOS.Class']/Installable
Languages$", GetValue("InstallableLanguages", obj));

oInst.AddProperty("$MPElement[Name='PlanetMPs.Win32_BIOS.Class']/InstallDate
$", GetValue("InstallDate", obj));

oInst.AddProperty("$MPElement[Name='PlanetMPs.Win32_BIOS.Class']/LanguageE
dition$", GetValue("LanguageEdition", obj));

oInst.AddProperty("$MPElement[Name='PlanetMPs.Win32_BIOS.Class']/ListOfLang
uages$", GetValue("ListOfLanguages", obj));

oInst.AddProperty("$MPElement[Name='PlanetMPs.Win32_BIOS.Class']/Manufactu
rer$", GetValue("Manufacturer", obj));

oInst.AddProperty("$MPElement[Name='PlanetMPs.Win32_BIOS.Class']/Name$",
GetValue("Name", obj));

oInst.AddProperty("$MPElement[Name='PlanetMPs.Win32_BIOS.Class']/OtherTarge
tOS$", GetValue("OtherTargetOS", obj));

oInst.AddProperty("$MPElement[Name='PlanetMPs.Win32_BIOS.Class']/PrimaryBI
OS$", GetValue("PrimaryBIOS", obj));

oInst.AddProperty("$MPElement[Name='PlanetMPs.Win32_BIOS.Class']/ReleaseDat
e$", GetValue("ReleaseDate", obj));

oInst.AddProperty("$MPElement[Name='PlanetMPs.Win32_BIOS.Class']/SerialNum
ber$", GetValue("SerialNumber", obj));

oInst.AddProperty("$MPElement[Name='PlanetMPs.Win32_BIOS.Class']/SMBIOSBI
OSVersion$", GetValue("SMBIOSBIOSVersion", obj));

oInst.AddProperty("$MPElement[Name='PlanetMPs.Win32_BIOS.Class']/SMBIOSMa
jorVersion$", GetValue("SMBIOSMajorVersion", obj));

oInst.AddProperty("$MPElement[Name='PlanetMPs.Win32_BIOS.Class']/SMBIOSMi
norVersion$", GetValue("SMBIOSMinorVersion", obj));
```

```
oInst.AddProperty("$MPElement[Name='PlanetMPs.Win32_BIOS.Class']/SMBIOSPre
sent$", GetValue("SMBIOSPresent", obj));

oInst.AddProperty("$MPElement[Name='PlanetMPs.Win32_BIOS.Class']/SoftwareEl
ementID$", GetValue("SoftwareElementID", obj));

oInst.AddProperty("$MPElement[Name='PlanetMPs.Win32_BIOS.Class']/SoftwareEl
ementState$", GetValue("SoftwareElementState", obj));

oInst.AddProperty("$MPElement[Name='PlanetMPs.Win32_BIOS.Class']/Status$",
GetValue("Status", obj));

oInst.AddProperty("$MPElement[Name='PlanetMPs.Win32_BIOS.Class']/TargetOper
atingSystem$", GetValue("TargetOperatingSystem", obj));

oInst.AddProperty("$MPElement[Name='PlanetMPs.Win32_BIOS.Class']/Version$",
GetValue("Version", obj));
                break;
        }
        oDiscoveryData.AddInstance(oInst);
        oAPI.Return(oDiscoveryData);
        function GetValue(Name, obj)
        {
            var tempstr = new String();
            var tempstr1 = new String();
            var tName = new String();
            tempstr1 = obj.GetObjectText_();
            var re = /"/g;
            tempstr1 = tempstr1.replace(re , "");
            var pos;
            tName = Name + " = ";
            pos = tempstr1.indexOf(tName);
            if (pos &gt; -1)
            {
               pos = pos + tName.length;
               tempstr = tempstr1.substring(pos, tempstr1.length);
               pos = tempstr.indexOf(";");
               tempstr = tempstr.substring(0, pos);
               tempstr = tempstr.replace("{", "");
```

```
                    tempstr = tempstr.replace("}", "");
                    if (tempstr.length &gt; 13)
                    {
                        if (obj.Properties_(Name).CIMType == 101)
                        {
                            tempstr = tempstr.substr(4, 2) + "/" + tempstr.substr(6, 2) +
"/" + tempstr.substr(0, 3) + " " + tempstr.substr(8, 2) + ":" + tempstr.substr(10, 2) +
":" + tempstr.substr(12, 2);
                        }
                    }
                    return tempstr;
                }
                else
                {
                    return "";
                }
            }
        </ScriptBody>
```

The ProbeAction ModuleType already gets the following three when passed into the DataSource:

```
<ScriptName>$Config/ScriptName$</ScriptName>
<Arguments>$Config/Arguments$</Arguments>
<ScriptBody>$Config/ScriptBody$</ScriptBody>
```

It gets the gets the following two from the DataSource itself:

```
<SecureInput>$Config/SecureInput$</SecureInput>
<EventPolicy>$Config/EventPolicy$</EventPolicy>
```

But we have to set the timeout:

```
<TimeoutSeconds>$Config/TimeoutSeconds$</TimeoutSeconds>
```

```
        <TimeoutSeconds>120</TimeoutSeconds>
    </DataSource>
</Discovery>
```

So, the discovery is set to run once a day. 60x60x24 = 8640 and is set to timeout for 120 seconds or 2 minutes.

Views and Folders

Here, we're adding 1 View, 1 folder and 1 Folder Item. From a view perspective, it would look like this:

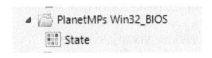

The View itself, can be one of the following:

Alert View
Event View
State View
Performance View
Diagram View
Task Status View
Web Page View
Dashboard View

Each are specified as follows:

TypeID="SC!Microsoft.SystemCenter.AlertViewType"
TypeID="SC!Microsoft.SystemCenter.EventViewType"
TypeID="SC!Microsoft.SystemCenter.StateViewType"
TypeID="SC!Microsoft.SystemCenter.PerformanceViewType"
TypeID="SC!Microsoft.SystemCenter.DiagramViewType"
TypeID="SC!Microsoft.SystemCenter.TaskStatusViewType"
TypeID="SC!Microsoft.SystemCenter.WebPageViewType"
TypeID="SC!Microsoft.SystemCenter.DaskboardViewType"

```
<Presentation>
 <Views>
  <View ID="PlanetMPs.Win32_BIOS.Class.Discovery.StateView"
Accessibility="Internal" Enabled="true" Target="PlanetMPs.Win32_BIOS.Class"
TypeID="SC!Microsoft.SystemCenter.StateViewType" Visible="true">
```

```
      <Category>Operations</Category><Criteria /></View>
    </Views>
    <Folders>
```

The Folder Element will also reference the System Center Library.

```
ParentFolder="SC!Microsoft.SystemCenter.Monitoring.ViewFolder.Root"
```

```
      <Folder ID="PlanetMPs.Win32_BIOS.ManagementPack.ViewFolder.Root"
Accessibility="Internal"
ParentFolder="SC!Microsoft.SystemCenter.Monitoring.ViewFolder.Root" />
    </Folders>
    <FolderItems>
      <FolderItem ElementID="PlanetMPs.Win32_BIOS.Class.Discovery.StateView"
Folder="PlanetMPs.Win32_BIOS.ManagementPack.ViewFolder.Root" />
    </FolderItems>
  </Presentation>
```

Well, we're almost done! We just have to cover the Display Strings

Language Packs and Display Strings

```
  <LanguagePacks>
   <LanguagePack ID="ENU" IsDefault="true">
    <DisplayStrings>
```

This string mirrors the Management Pack

```
    <DisplayString ElementID="PlanetMPs.Win32_BIOS.ManagementPack">
     <Name>PlanetMPs Win32_BIOS ManagementPack</Name>
     <Description>Discovers Win32_BIOS</Description>
    </DisplayString>
```

This string mirrors the Class we created.

```
    <DisplayString ElementID="PlanetMPs.Win32_BIOS.Class">
     <Name>PlanetMPs Win32_BIOS</Name>
```

```
    <Description>Creates A SQL table for PlanetMPs Win32_BIOS where
discovery information will be stored.</Description>
        </DisplayString>
```

This string mirrors the Discovery we created.

```
        <DisplayString ElementID="PlanetMPs.Win32_BIOS.Class.Discovery">
        <Name>PlanetMPs Win32_BIOS  Class Discovery</Name>
        <Description>Discovers and populates the SQL table for PlanetMPs
Win32_BIOS</Description>
        </DisplayString>
```

These are for displaying the Class' Properties correctly.

```
        <DisplayString ElementID="PlanetMPs.Win32_BIOS.Class"
SubElementID="BiosCharacteristics">
        <Name>BiosCharacteristics</Name>
        </DisplayString>
        <DisplayString ElementID="PlanetMPs.Win32_BIOS.Class"
SubElementID="BIOSVersion">
        <Name>BIOSVersion</Name>
        </DisplayString>
        <DisplayString ElementID="PlanetMPs.Win32_BIOS.Class"
SubElementID="BuildNumber">
        <Name>BuildNumber</Name>
        </DisplayString>
        <DisplayString ElementID="PlanetMPs.Win32_BIOS.Class"
SubElementID="Caption">
        <Name>Caption</Name>
        </DisplayString>
        <DisplayString ElementID="PlanetMPs.Win32_BIOS.Class"
SubElementID="CodeSet">
        <Name>CodeSet</Name>
        </DisplayString>
        <DisplayString ElementID="PlanetMPs.Win32_BIOS.Class"
SubElementID="CurrentLanguage">
        <Name>CurrentLanguage</Name>
        </DisplayString>
        <DisplayString ElementID="PlanetMPs.Win32_BIOS.Class"
SubElementID="Description">
```

```xml
        <Name>Description</Name>
        </DisplayString>
        <DisplayString ElementID="PlanetMPs.Win32_BIOS.Class"
SubElementID="IdentificationCode">
        <Name>IdentificationCode</Name>
        </DisplayString>
        <DisplayString ElementID="PlanetMPs.Win32_BIOS.Class"
SubElementID="InstallableLanguages">
        <Name>InstallableLanguages</Name>
        </DisplayString>
        <DisplayString ElementID="PlanetMPs.Win32_BIOS.Class"
SubElementID="InstallDate">
        <Name>InstallDate</Name>
        </DisplayString>
        <DisplayString ElementID="PlanetMPs.Win32_BIOS.Class"
SubElementID="LanguageEdition">
        <Name>LanguageEdition</Name>
        </DisplayString>
        <DisplayString ElementID="PlanetMPs.Win32_BIOS.Class"
SubElementID="ListOfLanguages">
        <Name>ListOfLanguages</Name>
        </DisplayString>
        <DisplayString ElementID="PlanetMPs.Win32_BIOS.Class"
SubElementID="Manufacturer">
        <Name>Manufacturer</Name>
        </DisplayString>
        <DisplayString ElementID="PlanetMPs.Win32_BIOS.Class"
SubElementID="Name">
        <Name>Name</Name>
        </DisplayString>
        <DisplayString ElementID="PlanetMPs.Win32_BIOS.Class"
SubElementID="OtherTargetOS">
        <Name>OtherTargetOS</Name>
        </DisplayString>
        <DisplayString ElementID="PlanetMPs.Win32_BIOS.Class"
SubElementID="PrimaryBIOS">
        <Name>PrimaryBIOS</Name>
        </DisplayString>
        <DisplayString ElementID="PlanetMPs.Win32_BIOS.Class"
SubElementID="ReleaseDate">
```

```xml
          <Name>ReleaseDate</Name>
        </DisplayString>
        <DisplayString ElementID="PlanetMPs.Win32_BIOS.Class"
SubElementID="SerialNumber">
          <Name>SerialNumber</Name>
        </DisplayString>
        <DisplayString ElementID="PlanetMPs.Win32_BIOS.Class"
SubElementID="SMBIOSBIOSVersion">
          <Name>SMBIOSBIOSVersion</Name>
        </DisplayString>
        <DisplayString ElementID="PlanetMPs.Win32_BIOS.Class"
SubElementID="SMBIOSMajorVersion">
          <Name>SMBIOSMajorVersion</Name>
        </DisplayString>
        <DisplayString ElementID="PlanetMPs.Win32_BIOS.Class"
SubElementID="SMBIOSMinorVersion">
          <Name>SMBIOSMinorVersion</Name>
        </DisplayString>
        <DisplayString ElementID="PlanetMPs.Win32_BIOS.Class"
SubElementID="SMBIOSPresent">
          <Name>SMBIOSPresent</Name>
        </DisplayString>
        <DisplayString ElementID="PlanetMPs.Win32_BIOS.Class"
SubElementID="SoftwareElementID">
          <Name>SoftwareElementID</Name>
        </DisplayString>
        <DisplayString ElementID="PlanetMPs.Win32_BIOS.Class"
SubElementID="SoftwareElementState">
          <Name>SoftwareElementState</Name>
        </DisplayString>
        <DisplayString ElementID="PlanetMPs.Win32_BIOS.Class"
SubElementID="Status">
          <Name>Status</Name>
        </DisplayString>
        <DisplayString ElementID="PlanetMPs.Win32_BIOS.Class"
SubElementID="TargetOperatingSystem">
          <Name>TargetOperatingSystem</Name>
        </DisplayString>
        <DisplayString ElementID="PlanetMPs.Win32_BIOS.Class"
SubElementID="Version">
```

```
    <Name>Version</Name>
  </DisplayString>
```

This is for the Discovery.StateView:

```
    <DisplayString
ElementID="PlanetMPs.Win32_BIOS.Class.Discovery.StateView">
      <Name>State</Name>
      <Description>Discovers and displays information for
Win32_BIOS</Description>
    </DisplayString>
```

This is for the ViewFolder.Root:

```
    <DisplayString
ElementID="PlanetMPs.Win32_BIOS.ManagementPack.ViewFolder.Root">
      <Name>PlanetMPs Win32_BIOS</Name>
    </DisplayString>
    </DisplayStrings>
  </LanguagePack>
</LanguagePacks>
```

And there you have it.

After being imported, SQL Server has now a table for Win32_BIOS information and now, we can use that table to create a lot of different reports including the SRS report in RDL format.

SQL Server and the SRS Report

Chapter Subtitle

Below is an example of how you can create SRS reports.

First, lets figure out where the table was created:

In the SCOM Console, we see this:

To Create the report, I created a connection string to SQL Server and queried MT_PlanetMPs$Win32_BIOS$Class, adjusted the sizes of the fields and got rid of all the GUIDs that made the report look ugly and unprofessional. Below is what the RDL file looks like:

```
<?xml version="1.0" encoding="utf-8"?>
<Report
xmlns:rd="http://schemas.microsoft.com/SQLServer/reporting/reportdesigner"
xmlns:cl="http://schemas.microsoft.com/sqlserver/reporting/2010/01/componentdef
inition"
xmlns="http://schemas.microsoft.com/sqlserver/reporting/2010/01/reportdefinition
">
<AutoRefresh>0</AutoRefresh>
<DataSources>
  <DataSource Name="DataSource1">
   <ConnectionProperties>
```

```xml
    <DataProvider>SQL</DataProvider>
    <ConnectString>Data Source = WIN-VNQ7KUKQ4NE;Integrated
Security=sspi;Initial Catalog=OperationsManager;</ConnectString>
    <IntegratedSecurity>true</IntegratedSecurity>
    </ConnectionProperties>
    <rd:SecurityType>Integrated</rd:SecurityType>
    <rd:DataSourceID>9d1bed3f-00d1-461b-9444-b0ed3d8268c6</rd:DataSourceID>
    </DataSource>
</DataSources>
<DataSets>
  <DataSet Name="DataSet1">
    <Query>
    <DataSourceName>DataSource1</DataSourceName>
    <CommandText>Select * from
dbo.MT_PlanetMPs$Win32_BIOS$Class</CommandText>
    <rd:UseGenericDesigner>true</rd:UseGenericDesigner>
    </Query>
    <Fields>
    <Field Name="BaseManagedEntityId">
      <DataField>BaseManagedEntityId</DataField>
      <rd:TypeName>System.String</rd:TypeName>
    </Field>
    <Field Name="BiosCharacteristics">

<DataField>BiosCharacteristics_1C92F61D_0FA6_3C9F_71C4_A67C162D16C1</Data
Field>
      <rd:TypeName>System.String</rd:TypeName>
    </Field>
    <Field Name="BIOSVersion">

<DataField>BIOSVersion_41F7989B_ADD1_41F7_DFBB_3230263337D3</DataField>
      <rd:TypeName>System.String</rd:TypeName>
    </Field>
    <Field Name="Caption">
      <DataField>Caption_C3CE76FE_01B5_7F17_1278_DB4F07B2DC33</DataField>
      <rd:TypeName>System.String</rd:TypeName>
    </Field>
    <Field Name="CurrentLanguage">

<DataField>CurrentLanguage_F1A4E0C3_F5EA_2739_E6DF_14E730481E22</DataF
ield>
      <rd:TypeName>System.String</rd:TypeName>
    </Field>
    <Field Name="Description">

<DataField>Description_59FBC381_993C_29F3_2192_BBA90136E14A</DataField>
      <rd:TypeName>System.String</rd:TypeName>
    </Field>
    <Field Name="InstallableLanguages">
```

```xml
<DataField>InstallableLanguages_FB97773A_9188_8A33_9485_E974F32087E8</D
ataField>
    <rd:TypeName>System.String</rd:TypeName>
    </Field>
    <Field Name="ListOfLanguages">

<DataField>ListOfLanguages_F47495B4_7189_F3D8_888A_27AA1A248FF4</DataF
ield>
    <rd:TypeName>System.String</rd:TypeName>
    </Field>
    <Field Name="Manufacturer">

<DataField>Manufacturer_53B4B96F_C3BB_87B5_2B6F_7C6416E39EAA</DataFiel
d>
    <rd:TypeName>System.String</rd:TypeName>
    </Field>
    <Field Name="Name">
     <DataField>Name_DA5532A5_165C_F1F5_BE68_4F53C316BFBD</DataField>
     <rd:TypeName>System.String</rd:TypeName>
    </Field>
    <Field Name="ObjectStatus">

<DataField>ObjectStatus_4AE3E5FE_BC03_1336_0A45_80BF58DEE57B</DataField
>
    <rd:TypeName>System.String</rd:TypeName>
    </Field>
    <Field Name="PrimaryBIOS">

<DataField>PrimaryBIOS_D0F3535A_C015_BFAB_E913_1E50DCE0F6B1</DataField
>
    <rd:TypeName>System.String</rd:TypeName>
    </Field>
    <Field Name="ReleaseDate">

<DataField>ReleaseDate_5A18E38F_A8C7_0F71_6FEC_AE3AC8370276</DataField>
    <rd:TypeName>System.String</rd:TypeName>
    </Field>
    <Field Name="SerialNumber">

<DataField>SerialNumber_5C1AE86E_EECF_A723_B9B2_3A81599F9CB4</DataFiel
d>
    <rd:TypeName>System.String</rd:TypeName>
    </Field>
    <Field Name="SMBIOSBIOSVersion">

<DataField>SMBIOSBIOSVersion_9F466916_2FA5_17CE_DDDA_FF0780C5290C</D
ataField>
    <rd:TypeName>System.String</rd:TypeName>
    </Field>
```

```xml
<Field Name="SMBIOSMajorVersion">

<DataField>SMBIOSMajorVersion_A180070C_25FF_00B1_8D84_EE64F39F2B43</DataField>
    <rd:TypeName>System.String</rd:TypeName>
    </Field>
    <Field Name="SMBIOSMinorVersion">

<DataField>SMBIOSMinorVersion_B5171766_53DD_E307_9519_E8A11CFB842B</DataField>
    <rd:TypeName>System.String</rd:TypeName>
    </Field>
    <Field Name="SMBIOSPresent">

<DataField>SMBIOSPresent_907D9A8C_B2C2_C7CC_BCF2_CA971609D3CC</DataField>
    <rd:TypeName>System.String</rd:TypeName>
    </Field>
    <Field Name="SoftwareElementID">

<DataField>SoftwareElementID_48A0A05C_C9AF_E596_B372_66FE4F23302D</DataField>
    <rd:TypeName>System.String</rd:TypeName>
    </Field>
    <Field Name="SoftwareElementState">

<DataField>SoftwareElementState_CD4749D4_20EF_12AC_7CB3_50018D5D9AB0</DataField>
    <rd:TypeName>System.String</rd:TypeName>
    </Field>
    <Field Name="Status">
    <DataField>Status_A0700E4E_A205_4BB2_1B1A_15C5282B1AF0</DataField>
    <rd:TypeName>System.String</rd:TypeName>
    </Field>
    <Field Name="TargetOperatingSystem">

<DataField>TargetOperatingSystem_F5894BED_96E3_1805_8518_D579BE31634D</DataField>
    <rd:TypeName>System.String</rd:TypeName>
    </Field>
    <Field Name="Version">

<DataField>Version_3854D8DB_16A5_3A62_8F5D_A2A7E7FBB065</DataField>
    <rd:TypeName>System.String</rd:TypeName>
    </Field>
   </Fields>
  </DataSet>
 </DataSets>
 <ReportSections>
  <ReportSection>
```

```xml
<Body>
 <ReportItems>
  <Tablix Name="Tablix1">
   <TablixBody>
    <TablixColumns>
     <TablixColumn>
      <Width>3in</Width>
     </TablixColumn>
     <TablixColumn>
      <Width>10in</Width>
     </TablixColumn>
     <TablixColumn>
      <Width>9in</Width>
     </TablixColumn>
     <TablixColumn>
      <Width>4in</Width>
     </TablixColumn>
     <TablixColumn>
      <Width>2in</Width>
     </TablixColumn>
     <TablixColumn>
      <Width>4in</Width>
     </TablixColumn>
     <TablixColumn>
      <Width>2in</Width>
     </TablixColumn>
     <TablixColumn>
      <Width>10in</Width>
     </TablixColumn>
     <TablixColumn>
      <Width>2in</Width>
     </TablixColumn>
     <TablixColumn>
      <Width>4in</Width>
     </TablixColumn>
     <TablixColumn>
      <Width>3in</Width>
     </TablixColumn>
     <TablixColumn>
      <Width>1.5in</Width>
     </TablixColumn>
     <TablixColumn>
      <Width>2in</Width>
     </TablixColumn>
     <TablixColumn>
      <Width>2in</Width>
     </TablixColumn>
     <TablixColumn>
      <Width>2in</Width>
     </TablixColumn>
```

```xml
<TablixColumn>
  <Width>2in</Width>
</TablixColumn>
<TablixColumn>
  <Width>2in</Width>
</TablixColumn>
<TablixColumn>
  <Width>2in</Width>
</TablixColumn>
<TablixColumn>
  <Width>4in</Width>
</TablixColumn>
<TablixColumn>
  <Width>2in</Width>
</TablixColumn>
<TablixColumn>
  <Width>1.5in</Width>
</TablixColumn>
<TablixColumn>
  <Width>2in</Width>
</TablixColumn>
<TablixColumn>
  <Width>9in</Width>
</TablixColumn>
</TablixColumns>
<TablixRows>
  <TablixRow>
    <Height>0.25in</Height>
    <TablixCells>
      <TablixCell>
        <CellContents>
          <Textbox Name="BaseManagedEntityId">
            <CanGrow>true</CanGrow>
            <KeepTogether>true</KeepTogether>
            <Paragraphs>
              <Paragraph>
                <TextRuns>
                  <TextRun>
                    <Value>BaseManagedEntityId</Value>
                    <Style>
                      <FontFamily>Tahoma</FontFamily>
                      <FontSize>11pt</FontSize>
                      <FontWeight>Bold</FontWeight>
                      <Color>White</Color>
                    </Style>
                  </TextRun>
                </TextRuns>
                <Style />
              </Paragraph>
            </Paragraphs>
```

```xml
      <rd:DefaultName>BaseManagedEntityId</rd:DefaultName>
      <Style>
       <Border>
        <Color>#7292cc</Color>
        <Style>Solid</Style>
       </Border>
       <BackgroundColor>#4c68a2</BackgroundColor>
       <PaddingLeft>2pt</PaddingLeft>
       <PaddingRight>2pt</PaddingRight>
       <PaddingTop>2pt</PaddingTop>
       <PaddingBottom>2pt</PaddingBottom>
      </Style>
     </Textbox>
    </CellContents>
   </TablixCell>
   <TablixCell>
    <CellContents>
     <Textbox Name="BiosCharacteristics">
      <CanGrow>true</CanGrow>
      <KeepTogether>true</KeepTogether>
      <Paragraphs>
       <Paragraph>
        <TextRuns>
         <TextRun>
          <Value>BiosCharacteristics</Value>
          <Style>
           <FontFamily>Tahoma</FontFamily>
           <FontSize>11pt</FontSize>
           <FontWeight>Bold</FontWeight>
           <Color>White</Color>
          </Style>
         </TextRun>
        </TextRuns>
        <Style />
       </Paragraph>
      </Paragraphs>
      <rd:DefaultName>BiosCharacteristics</rd:DefaultName>
      <Style>
       <Border>
        <Color>#7292cc</Color>
        <Style>Solid</Style>
       </Border>
       <BackgroundColor>#4c68a2</BackgroundColor>
       <PaddingLeft>2pt</PaddingLeft>
       <PaddingRight>2pt</PaddingRight>
       <PaddingTop>2pt</PaddingTop>
       <PaddingBottom>2pt</PaddingBottom>
      </Style>
     </Textbox>
    </CellContents>
```

```xml
        </TablixCell>
        <TablixCell>
         <CellContents>
          <Textbox Name="BIOSVersion">
           <CanGrow>true</CanGrow>
           <KeepTogether>true</KeepTogether>
           <Paragraphs>
            <Paragraph>
             <TextRuns>
              <TextRun>
               <Value>BIOSVersion</Value>
               <Style>
                <FontFamily>Tahoma</FontFamily>
                <FontSize>11pt</FontSize>
                <FontWeight>Bold</FontWeight>
                <Color>White</Color>
               </Style>
              </TextRun>
             </TextRuns>
             <Style />
            </Paragraph>
           </Paragraphs>
           <rd:DefaultName>BIOSVersion</rd:DefaultName>
           <Style>
            <Border>
             <Color>#7292cc</Color>
             <Style>Solid</Style>
            </Border>
            <BackgroundColor>#4c68a2</BackgroundColor>
            <PaddingLeft>2pt</PaddingLeft>
            <PaddingRight>2pt</PaddingRight>
            <PaddingTop>2pt</PaddingTop>
            <PaddingBottom>2pt</PaddingBottom>
           </Style>
          </Textbox>
         </CellContents>
        </TablixCell>
        <TablixCell>
         <CellContents>
          <Textbox Name="Caption">
           <CanGrow>true</CanGrow>
           <KeepTogether>true</KeepTogether>
           <Paragraphs>
            <Paragraph>
             <TextRuns>
              <TextRun>
               <Value>Caption</Value>
               <Style>
                <FontFamily>Tahoma</FontFamily>
                <FontSize>11pt</FontSize>
```

```xml
          <FontWeight>Bold</FontWeight>
          <Color>White</Color>
          </Style>
        </TextRun>
      </TextRuns>
      <Style />
    </Paragraph>
  </Paragraphs>
  <rd:DefaultName>Caption</rd:DefaultName>
  <Style>
    <Border>
      <Color>#7292cc</Color>
      <Style>Solid</Style>
    </Border>
    <BackgroundColor>#4c68a2</BackgroundColor>
    <PaddingLeft>2pt</PaddingLeft>
    <PaddingRight>2pt</PaddingRight>
    <PaddingTop>2pt</PaddingTop>
    <PaddingBottom>2pt</PaddingBottom>
  </Style>
  </Textbox>
  </CellContents>
</TablixCell>
<TablixCell>
  <CellContents>
    <Textbox Name="CurrentLanguage">
    <CanGrow>true</CanGrow>
    <KeepTogether>true</KeepTogether>
    <Paragraphs>
      <Paragraph>
        <TextRuns>
          <TextRun>
            <Value>CurrentLanguage</Value>
            <Style>
              <FontFamily>Tahoma</FontFamily>
              <FontSize>11pt</FontSize>
              <FontWeight>Bold</FontWeight>
              <Color>White</Color>
            </Style>
          </TextRun>
        </TextRuns>
        <Style />
      </Paragraph>
    </Paragraphs>
    <rd:DefaultName>CurrentLanguage</rd:DefaultName>
    <Style>
      <Border>
        <Color>#7292cc</Color>
        <Style>Solid</Style>
      </Border>
```

```xml
      <BackgroundColor>#4c68a2</BackgroundColor>
      <PaddingLeft>2pt</PaddingLeft>
      <PaddingRight>2pt</PaddingRight>
      <PaddingTop>2pt</PaddingTop>
      <PaddingBottom>2pt</PaddingBottom>
     </Style>
    </Textbox>
  </CellContents>
 </TablixCell>
<TablixCell>
 <CellContents>
   <Textbox Name="Description">
    <CanGrow>true</CanGrow>
    <KeepTogether>true</KeepTogether>
    <Paragraphs>
     <Paragraph>
      <TextRuns>
       <TextRun>
        <Value>Description</Value>
        <Style>
         <FontFamily>Tahoma</FontFamily>
         <FontSize>11pt</FontSize>
         <FontWeight>Bold</FontWeight>
         <Color>White</Color>
        </Style>
       </TextRun>
      </TextRuns>
      <Style />
     </Paragraph>
    </Paragraphs>
    <rd:DefaultName>Description</rd:DefaultName>
    <Style>
     <Border>
      <Color>#7292cc</Color>
      <Style>Solid</Style>
     </Border>
     <BackgroundColor>#4c68a2</BackgroundColor>
     <PaddingLeft>2pt</PaddingLeft>
     <PaddingRight>2pt</PaddingRight>
     <PaddingTop>2pt</PaddingTop>
     <PaddingBottom>2pt</PaddingBottom>
    </Style>
   </Textbox>
  </CellContents>
 </TablixCell>
<TablixCell>
 <CellContents>
   <Textbox Name="InstallableLanguages">
    <CanGrow>true</CanGrow>
    <KeepTogether>true</KeepTogether>
```

```xml
<Paragraphs>
 <Paragraph>
  <TextRuns>
   <TextRun>
    <Value>InstallableLanguages</Value>
    <Style>
     <FontFamily>Tahoma</FontFamily>
     <FontSize>11pt</FontSize>
     <FontWeight>Bold</FontWeight>
     <Color>White</Color>
    </Style>
   </TextRun>
  </TextRuns>
  <Style />
 </Paragraph>
</Paragraphs>
<rd:DefaultName>InstallableLanguages</rd:DefaultName>
<Style>
 <Border>
  <Color>#7292cc</Color>
  <Style>Solid</Style>
 </Border>
 <BackgroundColor>#4c68a2</BackgroundColor>
 <PaddingLeft>2pt</PaddingLeft>
 <PaddingRight>2pt</PaddingRight>
 <PaddingTop>2pt</PaddingTop>
 <PaddingBottom>2pt</PaddingBottom>
</Style>
</Textbox>
</CellContents>
</TablixCell>
<TablixCell>
 <CellContents>
  <Textbox Name="ListOfLanguages">
  <CanGrow>true</CanGrow>
  <KeepTogether>true</KeepTogether>
  <Paragraphs>
   <Paragraph>
    <TextRuns>
     <TextRun>
      <Value>ListOfLanguages</Value>
      <Style>
       <FontFamily>Tahoma</FontFamily>
       <FontSize>11pt</FontSize>
       <FontWeight>Bold</FontWeight>
       <Color>White</Color>
      </Style>
     </TextRun>
    </TextRuns>
    <Style />
```

```xml
          </Paragraph>
         </Paragraphs>
         <rd:DefaultName>ListOfLanguages</rd:DefaultName>
         <Style>
          <Border>
           <Color>#7292cc</Color>
           <Style>Solid</Style>
          </Border>
          <BackgroundColor>#4c68a2</BackgroundColor>
          <PaddingLeft>2pt</PaddingLeft>
          <PaddingRight>2pt</PaddingRight>
          <PaddingTop>2pt</PaddingTop>
          <PaddingBottom>2pt</PaddingBottom>
         </Style>
        </Textbox>
       </CellContents>
      </TablixCell>
      <TablixCell>
       <CellContents>
        <Textbox Name="Manufacturer">
         <CanGrow>true</CanGrow>
         <KeepTogether>true</KeepTogether>
         <Paragraphs>
          <Paragraph>
           <TextRuns>
            <TextRun>
             <Value>Manufacturer</Value>
             <Style>
              <FontFamily>Tahoma</FontFamily>
              <FontSize>11pt</FontSize>
              <FontWeight>Bold</FontWeight>
              <Color>White</Color>
             </Style>
            </TextRun>
           </TextRuns>
           <Style />
          </Paragraph>
         </Paragraphs>
         <rd:DefaultName>Manufacturer</rd:DefaultName>
         <Style>
          <Border>
           <Color>#7292cc</Color>
           <Style>Solid</Style>
          </Border>
          <BackgroundColor>#4c68a2</BackgroundColor>
          <PaddingLeft>2pt</PaddingLeft>
          <PaddingRight>2pt</PaddingRight>
          <PaddingTop>2pt</PaddingTop>
          <PaddingBottom>2pt</PaddingBottom>
         </Style>
```

```xml
          </Textbox>
        </CellContents>
      </TablixCell>
      <TablixCell>
        <CellContents>
          <Textbox Name="Name">
            <CanGrow>true</CanGrow>
            <KeepTogether>true</KeepTogether>
            <Paragraphs>
              <Paragraph>
                <TextRuns>
                  <TextRun>
                    <Value>Name</Value>
                    <Style>
                      <FontFamily>Tahoma</FontFamily>
                      <FontSize>11pt</FontSize>
                      <FontWeight>Bold</FontWeight>
                      <Color>White</Color>
                    </Style>
                  </TextRun>
                </TextRuns>
                <Style />
              </Paragraph>
            </Paragraphs>
            <rd:DefaultName>Name</rd:DefaultName>
            <Style>
              <Border>
                <Color>#7292cc</Color>
                <Style>Solid</Style>
              </Border>
              <BackgroundColor>#4c68a2</BackgroundColor>
              <PaddingLeft>2pt</PaddingLeft>
              <PaddingRight>2pt</PaddingRight>
              <PaddingTop>2pt</PaddingTop>
              <PaddingBottom>2pt</PaddingBottom>
            </Style>
          </Textbox>
        </CellContents>
      </TablixCell>
      <TablixCell>
        <CellContents>
          <Textbox Name="ObjectStatus">
            <CanGrow>true</CanGrow>
            <KeepTogether>true</KeepTogether>
            <Paragraphs>
              <Paragraph>
                <TextRuns>
                  <TextRun>
                    <Value>ObjectStatus</Value>
                    <Style>
```

```xml
            <FontFamily>Tahoma</FontFamily>
            <FontSize>11pt</FontSize>
            <FontWeight>Bold</FontWeight>
            <Color>White</Color>
          </Style>
        </TextRun>
      </TextRuns>
      <Style />
    </Paragraph>
  </Paragraphs>
  <rd:DefaultName>ObjectStatus</rd:DefaultName>
  <Style>
    <Border>
      <Color>#7292cc</Color>
      <Style>Solid</Style>
    </Border>
    <BackgroundColor>#4c68a2</BackgroundColor>
    <PaddingLeft>2pt</PaddingLeft>
    <PaddingRight>2pt</PaddingRight>
    <PaddingTop>2pt</PaddingTop>
    <PaddingBottom>2pt</PaddingBottom>
  </Style>
  </Textbox>
 </CellContents>
</TablixCell>
<TablixCell>
 <CellContents>
  <Textbox Name="PrimaryBIOS">
  <CanGrow>true</CanGrow>
  <KeepTogether>true</KeepTogether>
  <Paragraphs>
   <Paragraph>
    <TextRuns>
     <TextRun>
      <Value>PrimaryBIOS</Value>
      <Style>
       <FontFamily>Tahoma</FontFamily>
       <FontSize>11pt</FontSize>
       <FontWeight>Bold</FontWeight>
       <Color>White</Color>
      </Style>
     </TextRun>
    </TextRuns>
    <Style />
   </Paragraph>
  </Paragraphs>
  <rd:DefaultName>PrimaryBIOS</rd:DefaultName>
  <Style>
   <Border>
    <Color>#7292cc</Color>
```

```xml
    <Style>Solid</Style>
   </Border>
   <BackgroundColor>#4c68a2</BackgroundColor>
   <PaddingLeft>2pt</PaddingLeft>
   <PaddingRight>2pt</PaddingRight>
   <PaddingTop>2pt</PaddingTop>
   <PaddingBottom>2pt</PaddingBottom>
  </Style>
 </Textbox>
</CellContents>
</TablixCell>
<TablixCell>
 <CellContents>
  <Textbox Name="ReleaseDate">
   <CanGrow>true</CanGrow>
   <KeepTogether>true</KeepTogether>
   <Paragraphs>
    <Paragraph>
     <TextRuns>
      <TextRun>
       <Value>ReleaseDate</Value>
       <Style>
        <FontFamily>Tahoma</FontFamily>
        <FontSize>11pt</FontSize>
        <FontWeight>Bold</FontWeight>
        <Color>White</Color>
       </Style>
      </TextRun>
     </TextRuns>
     <Style />
    </Paragraph>
   </Paragraphs>
   <rd:DefaultName>ReleaseDate</rd:DefaultName>
   <Style>
    <Border>
     <Color>#7292cc</Color>
     <Style>Solid</Style>
    </Border>
    <BackgroundColor>#4c68a2</BackgroundColor>
    <PaddingLeft>2pt</PaddingLeft>
    <PaddingRight>2pt</PaddingRight>
    <PaddingTop>2pt</PaddingTop>
    <PaddingBottom>2pt</PaddingBottom>
   </Style>
  </Textbox>
 </CellContents>
</TablixCell>
<TablixCell>
 <CellContents>
  <Textbox Name="SerialNumber">
```

```xml
        <CanGrow>true</CanGrow>
        <KeepTogether>true</KeepTogether>
        <Paragraphs>
         <Paragraph>
          <TextRuns>
           <TextRun>
            <Value>SerialNumber</Value>
            <Style>
             <FontFamily>Tahoma</FontFamily>
             <FontSize>11pt</FontSize>
             <FontWeight>Bold</FontWeight>
             <Color>White</Color>
            </Style>
           </TextRun>
          </TextRuns>
          <Style />
         </Paragraph>
        </Paragraphs>
        <rd:DefaultName>SerialNumber</rd:DefaultName>
        <Style>
         <Border>
          <Color>#7292cc</Color>
          <Style>Solid</Style>
         </Border>
         <BackgroundColor>#4c68a2</BackgroundColor>
         <PaddingLeft>2pt</PaddingLeft>
         <PaddingRight>2pt</PaddingRight>
         <PaddingTop>2pt</PaddingTop>
         <PaddingBottom>2pt</PaddingBottom>
        </Style>
       </Textbox>
      </CellContents>
     </TablixCell>
     <TablixCell>
      <CellContents>
       <Textbox Name="SMBIOSBIOSVersion">
        <CanGrow>true</CanGrow>
        <KeepTogether>true</KeepTogether>
        <Paragraphs>
         <Paragraph>
          <TextRuns>
           <TextRun>
            <Value>SMBIOSBIOSVersion</Value>
            <Style>
             <FontFamily>Tahoma</FontFamily>
             <FontSize>11pt</FontSize>
             <FontWeight>Bold</FontWeight>
             <Color>White</Color>
            </Style>
           </TextRun>
```

```xml
      </TextRuns>
      <Style />
    </Paragraph>
  </Paragraphs>
  <rd:DefaultName>SMBIOSBIOSVersion</rd:DefaultName>
  <Style>
    <Border>
      <Color>#7292cc</Color>
      <Style>Solid</Style>
    </Border>
    <BackgroundColor>#4c68a2</BackgroundColor>
    <PaddingLeft>2pt</PaddingLeft>
    <PaddingRight>2pt</PaddingRight>
    <PaddingTop>2pt</PaddingTop>
    <PaddingBottom>2pt</PaddingBottom>
  </Style>
  </Textbox>
 </CellContents>
</TablixCell>
<TablixCell>
 <CellContents>
  <Textbox Name="SMBIOSMajorVersion">
  <CanGrow>true</CanGrow>
  <KeepTogether>true</KeepTogether>
  <Paragraphs>
    <Paragraph>
     <TextRuns>
      <TextRun>
       <Value>SMBIOSMajorVersion</Value>
       <Style>
        <FontFamily>Tahoma</FontFamily>
        <FontSize>11pt</FontSize>
        <FontWeight>Bold</FontWeight>
        <Color>White</Color>
       </Style>
      </TextRun>
     </TextRuns>
     <Style />
    </Paragraph>
  </Paragraphs>
  <rd:DefaultName>SMBIOSMajorVersion</rd:DefaultName>
  <Style>
    <Border>
      <Color>#7292cc</Color>
      <Style>Solid</Style>
    </Border>
    <BackgroundColor>#4c68a2</BackgroundColor>
    <PaddingLeft>2pt</PaddingLeft>
    <PaddingRight>2pt</PaddingRight>
    <PaddingTop>2pt</PaddingTop>
```

```
        <PaddingBottom>2pt</PaddingBottom>
      </Style>
    </Textbox>
  </CellContents>
</TablixCell>
<TablixCell>
  <CellContents>
    <Textbox Name="SMBIOSMinorVersion">
      <CanGrow>true</CanGrow>
      <KeepTogether>true</KeepTogether>
      <Paragraphs>
        <Paragraph>
          <TextRuns>
            <TextRun>
              <Value>SMBIOSMinorVersion</Value>
              <Style>
                <FontFamily>Tahoma</FontFamily>
                <FontSize>11pt</FontSize>
                <FontWeight>Bold</FontWeight>
                <Color>White</Color>
              </Style>
            </TextRun>
          </TextRuns>
          <Style />
        </Paragraph>
      </Paragraphs>
      <rd:DefaultName>SMBIOSMinorVersion</rd:DefaultName>
      <Style>
        <Border>
          <Color>#7292cc</Color>
          <Style>Solid</Style>
        </Border>
        <BackgroundColor>#4c68a2</BackgroundColor>
        <PaddingLeft>2pt</PaddingLeft>
        <PaddingRight>2pt</PaddingRight>
        <PaddingTop>2pt</PaddingTop>
        <PaddingBottom>2pt</PaddingBottom>
      </Style>
    </Textbox>
  </CellContents>
</TablixCell>
<TablixCell>
  <CellContents>
    <Textbox Name="SMBIOSPresent">
      <CanGrow>true</CanGrow>
      <KeepTogether>true</KeepTogether>
      <Paragraphs>
        <Paragraph>
          <TextRuns>
            <TextRun>
```

```xml
          <Value>SMBIOSPresent</Value>
          <Style>
           <FontFamily>Tahoma</FontFamily>
           <FontSize>11pt</FontSize>
           <FontWeight>Bold</FontWeight>
           <Color>White</Color>
          </Style>
         </TextRun>
        </TextRuns>
        <Style />
       </Paragraph>
      </Paragraphs>
      <rd:DefaultName>SMBIOSPresent</rd:DefaultName>
      <Style>
       <Border>
        <Color>#7292cc</Color>
        <Style>Solid</Style>
       </Border>
       <BackgroundColor>#4c68a2</BackgroundColor>
       <PaddingLeft>2pt</PaddingLeft>
       <PaddingRight>2pt</PaddingRight>
       <PaddingTop>2pt</PaddingTop>
       <PaddingBottom>2pt</PaddingBottom>
      </Style>
     </Textbox>
    </CellContents>
   </TablixCell>
   <TablixCell>
    <CellContents>
     <Textbox Name="SoftwareElementID">
      <CanGrow>true</CanGrow>
      <KeepTogether>true</KeepTogether>
      <Paragraphs>
       <Paragraph>
        <TextRuns>
         <TextRun>
          <Value>SoftwareElementID</Value>
          <Style>
           <FontFamily>Tahoma</FontFamily>
           <FontSize>11pt</FontSize>
           <FontWeight>Bold</FontWeight>
           <Color>White</Color>
          </Style>
         </TextRun>
        </TextRuns>
        <Style />
       </Paragraph>
      </Paragraphs>
      <rd:DefaultName>SoftwareElementID</rd:DefaultName>
      <Style>
```

```xml
      <Border>
       <Color>#7292cc</Color>
       <Style>Solid</Style>
      </Border>
      <BackgroundColor>#4c68a2</BackgroundColor>
      <PaddingLeft>2pt</PaddingLeft>
      <PaddingRight>2pt</PaddingRight>
      <PaddingTop>2pt</PaddingTop>
      <PaddingBottom>2pt</PaddingBottom>
     </Style>
    </Textbox>
   </CellContents>
  </TablixCell>
  <TablixCell>
   <CellContents>
    <Textbox Name="SoftwareElementState">
     <CanGrow>true</CanGrow>
     <KeepTogether>true</KeepTogether>
     <Paragraphs>
      <Paragraph>
       <TextRuns>
        <TextRun>
         <Value>SoftwareElementState</Value>
         <Style>
          <FontFamily>Tahoma</FontFamily>
          <FontSize>11pt</FontSize>
          <FontWeight>Bold</FontWeight>
          <Color>White</Color>
         </Style>
        </TextRun>
       </TextRuns>
       <Style />
      </Paragraph>
     </Paragraphs>
     <rd:DefaultName>SoftwareElementState</rd:DefaultName>
     <Style>
      <Border>
       <Color>#7292cc</Color>
       <Style>Solid</Style>
      </Border>
      <BackgroundColor>#4c68a2</BackgroundColor>
      <PaddingLeft>2pt</PaddingLeft>
      <PaddingRight>2pt</PaddingRight>
      <PaddingTop>2pt</PaddingTop>
      <PaddingBottom>2pt</PaddingBottom>
     </Style>
    </Textbox>
   </CellContents>
  </TablixCell>
  <TablixCell>
```

```xml
<CellContents>
  <Textbox Name="Status">
   <CanGrow>true</CanGrow>
   <KeepTogether>true</KeepTogether>
   <Paragraphs>
    <Paragraph>
     <TextRuns>
      <TextRun>
       <Value>Status</Value>
       <Style>
        <FontFamily>Tahoma</FontFamily>
        <FontSize>11pt</FontSize>
        <FontWeight>Bold</FontWeight>
        <Color>White</Color>
       </Style>
      </TextRun>
     </TextRuns>
     <Style />
    </Paragraph>
   </Paragraphs>
   <rd:DefaultName>Status</rd:DefaultName>
   <Style>
    <Border>
     <Color>#7292cc</Color>
     <Style>Solid</Style>
    </Border>
    <BackgroundColor>#4c68a2</BackgroundColor>
    <PaddingLeft>2pt</PaddingLeft>
    <PaddingRight>2pt</PaddingRight>
    <PaddingTop>2pt</PaddingTop>
    <PaddingBottom>2pt</PaddingBottom>
   </Style>
  </Textbox>
 </CellContents>
</TablixCell>
<TablixCell>
 <CellContents>
  <Textbox Name="TargetOperatingSystem">
   <CanGrow>true</CanGrow>
   <KeepTogether>true</KeepTogether>
   <Paragraphs>
    <Paragraph>
     <TextRuns>
      <TextRun>
       <Value>TargetOperatingSystem</Value>
       <Style>
        <FontFamily>Tahoma</FontFamily>
        <FontSize>11pt</FontSize>
        <FontWeight>Bold</FontWeight>
        <Color>White</Color>
```

```xml
          </Style>
         </TextRun>
        </TextRuns>
        <Style />
       </Paragraph>
      </Paragraphs>
      <rd:DefaultName>TargetOperatingSystem</rd:DefaultName>
      <Style>
       <Border>
        <Color>#7292cc</Color>
        <Style>Solid</Style>
       </Border>
       <BackgroundColor>#4c68a2</BackgroundColor>
       <PaddingLeft>2pt</PaddingLeft>
       <PaddingRight>2pt</PaddingRight>
       <PaddingTop>2pt</PaddingTop>
       <PaddingBottom>2pt</PaddingBottom>
      </Style>
     </Textbox>
    </CellContents>
   </TablixCell>
   <TablixCell>
    <CellContents>
     <Textbox Name="Version">
      <CanGrow>true</CanGrow>
      <KeepTogether>true</KeepTogether>
      <Paragraphs>
       <Paragraph>
        <TextRuns>
         <TextRun>
          <Value>Version</Value>
          <Style>
           <FontFamily>Tahoma</FontFamily>
           <FontSize>11pt</FontSize>
           <FontWeight>Bold</FontWeight>
           <Color>White</Color>
          </Style>
         </TextRun>
        </TextRuns>
        <Style />
       </Paragraph>
      </Paragraphs>
      <rd:DefaultName>Version</rd:DefaultName>
      <Style>
       <Border>
        <Color>#7292cc</Color>
        <Style>Solid</Style>
       </Border>
       <BackgroundColor>#4c68a2</BackgroundColor>
       <PaddingLeft>2pt</PaddingLeft>
```

```xml
          <PaddingRight>2pt</PaddingRight>
          <PaddingTop>2pt</PaddingTop>
          <PaddingBottom>2pt</PaddingBottom>
         </Style>
        </Textbox>
       </CellContents>
      </TablixCell>
     </TablixCells>
    </TablixRow>
    <TablixRow>
     <Height>0.25in</Height>
     <TablixCells>
      <TablixCell>
       <CellContents>
        <Textbox Name="TBBaseManagedEntityId">
         <CanGrow>true</CanGrow>
         <KeepTogether>true</KeepTogether>
         <Paragraphs>
          <Paragraph>
           <TextRuns>
            <TextRun>
             <Value>=Fields!BaseManagedEntityId.Value</Value>
             <Style>
              <FontFamily>Tahoma</FontFamily>
              <Color>#4d4d4d</Color>
             </Style>
            </TextRun>
           </TextRuns>
           <Style />
          </Paragraph>
         </Paragraphs>
         <rd:DefaultName>TBBaseManagedEntityId</rd:DefaultName>
         <Style>
          <Border>
           <Color>#e5e5e5</Color>
           <Style>Solid</Style>
          </Border>
          <PaddingLeft>2pt</PaddingLeft>
          <PaddingRight>2pt</PaddingRight>
          <PaddingTop>2pt</PaddingTop>
          <PaddingBottom>2pt</PaddingBottom>
         </Style>
        </Textbox>
       </CellContents>
      </TablixCell>
      <TablixCell>
       <CellContents>
        <Textbox
Name="TBBiosCharacteristics_1C92F61D_0FA6_3C9F_71C4_A67C162D16C1">
         <CanGrow>true</CanGrow>
```

```
          <KeepTogether>true</KeepTogether>
          <Paragraphs>
           <Paragraph>
            <TextRuns>
             <TextRun>
              <Value>=Fields!BiosCharacteristics.Value</Value>
              <Style>
               <FontFamily>Tahoma</FontFamily>
               <Color>#4d4d4d</Color>
              </Style>
             </TextRun>
            </TextRuns>
            <Style />
           </Paragraph>
          </Paragraphs>

<rd:DefaultName>TBBiosCharacteristics_1C92F61D_0FA6_3C9F_71C4_A67C162D1
6C1</rd:DefaultName>
          <Style>
           <Border>
            <Color>#e5e5e5</Color>
            <Style>Solid</Style>
           </Border>
           <PaddingLeft>2pt</PaddingLeft>
           <PaddingRight>2pt</PaddingRight>
           <PaddingTop>2pt</PaddingTop>
           <PaddingBottom>2pt</PaddingBottom>
          </Style>
         </Textbox>
        </CellContents>
       </TablixCell>
      <TablixCell>
        <CellContents>
         <Textbox
Name="TBBIOSVersion_41F7989B_ADD1_41F7_DFBB_3230263337D3">
          <CanGrow>true</CanGrow>
          <KeepTogether>true</KeepTogether>
          <Paragraphs>
           <Paragraph>
            <TextRuns>
             <TextRun>
              <Value>=Fields!BIOSVersion.Value</Value>
              <Style>
               <FontFamily>Tahoma</FontFamily>
               <Color>#4d4d4d</Color>
              </Style>
             </TextRun>
            </TextRuns>
            <Style />
           </Paragraph>
```

```
                </Paragraphs>

<rd:DefaultName>TBBIOSVersion__41F7989B_ADD1_41F7_DFBB_3230263337D3</r
d:DefaultName>
                <Style>
                 <Border>
                  <Color>#e5e5e5</Color>
                  <Style>Solid</Style>
                 </Border>
                 <PaddingLeft>2pt</PaddingLeft>
                 <PaddingRight>2pt</PaddingRight>
                 <PaddingTop>2pt</PaddingTop>
                 <PaddingBottom>2pt</PaddingBottom>
                </Style>
               </Textbox>
              </CellContents>
             </TablixCell>
             <TablixCell>
              <CellContents>
               <Textbox
Name="TBCaption__C3CE76FE_01B5_7F17_1278_DB4F07B2DC33">
                <CanGrow>true</CanGrow>
                <KeepTogether>true</KeepTogether>
                <Paragraphs>
                 <Paragraph>
                  <TextRuns>
                   <TextRun>
                    <Value>=Fields!Caption.Value</Value>
                    <Style>
                     <FontFamily>Tahoma</FontFamily>
                     <Color>#4d4d4d</Color>
                    </Style>
                   </TextRun>
                  </TextRuns>
                  <Style />
                 </Paragraph>
                </Paragraphs>

<rd:DefaultName>TBCaption__C3CE76FE_01B5_7F17_1278_DB4F07B2DC33</rd:Def
aultName>
                <Style>
                 <Border>
                  <Color>#e5e5e5</Color>
                  <Style>Solid</Style>
                 </Border>
                 <PaddingLeft>2pt</PaddingLeft>
                 <PaddingRight>2pt</PaddingRight>
                 <PaddingTop>2pt</PaddingTop>
                 <PaddingBottom>2pt</PaddingBottom>
                </Style>
```

```xml
      </Textbox>
     </CellContents>
    </TablixCell>
    <TablixCell>
     <CellContents>
      <Textbox
Name="TBCurrentLanguage_F1A4E0C3_F5EA_2739_E6DF_14E730481E22">
       <CanGrow>true</CanGrow>
       <KeepTogether>true</KeepTogether>
       <Paragraphs>
        <Paragraph>
         <TextRuns>
          <TextRun>
           <Value>=Fields!CurrentLanguage.Value</Value>
           <Style>
            <FontFamily>Tahoma</FontFamily>
            <Color>#4d4d4d</Color>
           </Style>
          </TextRun>
         </TextRuns>
         <Style />
        </Paragraph>
       </Paragraphs>

<rd:DefaultName>TBCurrentLanguage_F1A4E0C3_F5EA_2739_E6DF_14E730481E2
2</rd:DefaultName>
       <Style>
        <Border>
         <Color>#e5e5e5</Color>
         <Style>Solid</Style>
        </Border>
        <PaddingLeft>2pt</PaddingLeft>
        <PaddingRight>2pt</PaddingRight>
        <PaddingTop>2pt</PaddingTop>
        <PaddingBottom>2pt</PaddingBottom>
       </Style>
      </Textbox>
     </CellContents>
    </TablixCell>
    <TablixCell>
     <CellContents>
      <Textbox
Name="TBDescription_59FBC381_993C_29F3_2192_BBA90136E14A">
       <CanGrow>true</CanGrow>
       <KeepTogether>true</KeepTogether>
       <Paragraphs>
        <Paragraph>
         <TextRuns>
          <TextRun>
           <Value>=Fields!Description.Value</Value>
```

```xml
            <Style>
             <FontFamily>Tahoma</FontFamily>
             <Color>#4d4d4d</Color>
            </Style>
           </TextRun>
          </TextRuns>
          <Style />
         </Paragraph>
        </Paragraphs>

<rd:DefaultName>TBDescription_59FBC381_993C_29F3_2192_BBA90136E14A</rd:
DefaultName>
            <Style>
             <Border>
              <Color>#e5e5e5</Color>
              <Style>Solid</Style>
             </Border>
             <PaddingLeft>2pt</PaddingLeft>
             <PaddingRight>2pt</PaddingRight>
             <PaddingTop>2pt</PaddingTop>
             <PaddingBottom>2pt</PaddingBottom>
            </Style>
           </Textbox>
          </CellContents>
         </TablixCell>
         <TablixCell>
          <CellContents>
           <Textbox
Name="TBInstallableLanguages_FB97773A_9188_8A33_9485_E974F32087E8">
            <CanGrow>true</CanGrow>
            <KeepTogether>true</KeepTogether>
            <Paragraphs>
             <Paragraph>
              <TextRuns>
               <TextRun>
                <Value>=Fields!InstallableLanguages.Value</Value>
                <Style>
                 <FontFamily>Tahoma</FontFamily>
                 <Color>#4d4d4d</Color>
                </Style>
               </TextRun>
              </TextRuns>
              <Style />
             </Paragraph>
            </Paragraphs>

<rd:DefaultName>TBInstallableLanguages_FB97773A_9188_8A33_9485_E974F320
87E8</rd:DefaultName>
            <Style>
             <Border>
```

```xml
        <Color>#e5e5e5</Color>
        <Style>Solid</Style>
       </Border>
       <PaddingLeft>2pt</PaddingLeft>
       <PaddingRight>2pt</PaddingRight>
       <PaddingTop>2pt</PaddingTop>
       <PaddingBottom>2pt</PaddingBottom>
      </Style>
     </Textbox>
    </CellContents>
   </TablixCell>
   <TablixCell>
    <CellContents>
     <Textbox
Name="TBListOfLanguages__F47495B4__7189__F3D8__888A__27AA1A248FF4">
        <CanGrow>true</CanGrow>
        <KeepTogether>true</KeepTogether>
        <Paragraphs>
         <Paragraph>
          <TextRuns>
           <TextRun>
            <Value>=Fields!ListOfLanguages.Value</Value>
            <Style>
             <FontFamily>Tahoma</FontFamily>
             <Color>#4d4d4d</Color>
            </Style>
           </TextRun>
          </TextRuns>
          <Style />
         </Paragraph>
        </Paragraphs>

<rd:DefaultName>TBListOfLanguages__F47495B4__7189__F3D8__888A__27AA1A248FF
4</rd:DefaultName>
        <Style>
         <Border>
          <Color>#e5e5e5</Color>
          <Style>Solid</Style>
         </Border>
         <PaddingLeft>2pt</PaddingLeft>
         <PaddingRight>2pt</PaddingRight>
         <PaddingTop>2pt</PaddingTop>
         <PaddingBottom>2pt</PaddingBottom>
        </Style>
      </Textbox>
     </CellContents>
    </TablixCell>
    <TablixCell>
     <CellContents>
```

```
            <Textbox
Name="TBManufacturer__53B4B96F__C3BB__87B5__2B6F__7C6416E39EAA">
              <CanGrow>true</CanGrow>
              <KeepTogether>true</KeepTogether>
              <Paragraphs>
               <Paragraph>
                <TextRuns>
                 <TextRun>
                  <Value>=Fields!Manufacturer.Value</Value>
                  <Style>
                   <FontFamily>Tahoma</FontFamily>
                   <Color>#4d4d4d</Color>
                  </Style>
                 </TextRun>
                </TextRuns>
                <Style />
               </Paragraph>
              </Paragraphs>

<rd:DefaultName>TBManufacturer__53B4B96F__C3BB__87B5__2B6F__7C6416E39EAA</rd:DefaultName>
              <Style>
               <Border>
                <Color>#e5e5e5</Color>
                <Style>Solid</Style>
               </Border>
               <PaddingLeft>2pt</PaddingLeft>
               <PaddingRight>2pt</PaddingRight>
               <PaddingTop>2pt</PaddingTop>
               <PaddingBottom>2pt</PaddingBottom>
              </Style>
             </Textbox>
            </CellContents>
           </TablixCell>
           <TablixCell>
            <CellContents>
             <Textbox
Name="TBName__DA5532A5__165C__F1F5__BE68__4F53C316BFBD">
              <CanGrow>true</CanGrow>
              <KeepTogether>true</KeepTogether>
              <Paragraphs>
               <Paragraph>
                <TextRuns>
                 <TextRun>
                  <Value>=Fields!Name.Value</Value>
                  <Style>
                   <FontFamily>Tahoma</FontFamily>
                   <Color>#4d4d4d</Color>
                  </Style>
                 </TextRun>
```

```xml
          </TextRuns>
          <Style />
         </Paragraph>
        </Paragraphs>

<rd:DefaultName>TBName_DA5532A5_165C_F1F5_BE68_4F53C316BFBD</rd:Defa
ultName>
         <Style>
          <Border>
           <Color>#e5e5e5</Color>
           <Style>Solid</Style>
          </Border>
          <PaddingLeft>2pt</PaddingLeft>
          <PaddingRight>2pt</PaddingRight>
          <PaddingTop>2pt</PaddingTop>
          <PaddingBottom>2pt</PaddingBottom>
         </Style>
        </Textbox>
       </CellContents>
      </TablixCell>
      <TablixCell>
       <CellContents>
        <Textbox
Name="TBObjectStatus_4AE3E5FE_BC03_1336_0A45_80BF58DEE57B">
         <CanGrow>true</CanGrow>
         <KeepTogether>true</KeepTogether>
         <Paragraphs>
          <Paragraph>
           <TextRuns>
            <TextRun>
             <Value>=Fields!ObjectStatus.Value</Value>
             <Style>
              <FontFamily>Tahoma</FontFamily>
              <Color>#4d4d4d</Color>
             </Style>
            </TextRun>
           </TextRuns>
           <Style />
          </Paragraph>
         </Paragraphs>

<rd:DefaultName>TBObjectStatus_4AE3E5FE_BC03_1336_0A45_80BF58DEE57B</r
d:DefaultName>
         <Style>
          <Border>
           <Color>#e5e5e5</Color>
           <Style>Solid</Style>
          </Border>
          <PaddingLeft>2pt</PaddingLeft>
          <PaddingRight>2pt</PaddingRight>
```

```xml
            <PaddingTop>2pt</PaddingTop>
            <PaddingBottom>2pt</PaddingBottom>
          </Style>
        </Textbox>
      </CellContents>
    </TablixCell>
    <TablixCell>
      <CellContents>
        <Textbox
Name="TBPrimaryBIOS_D0F3535A_C015_BFAB_E913_1E50DCE0F6B1">
          <CanGrow>true</CanGrow>
          <KeepTogether>true</KeepTogether>
          <Paragraphs>
            <Paragraph>
              <TextRuns>
                <TextRun>
                  <Value>=Fields!PrimaryBIOS.Value</Value>
                  <Style>
                    <FontFamily>Tahoma</FontFamily>
                    <Color>#4d4d4d</Color>
                  </Style>
                </TextRun>
              </TextRuns>
              <Style />
            </Paragraph>
          </Paragraphs>

<rd:DefaultName>TBPrimaryBIOS_D0F3535A_C015_BFAB_E913_1E50DCE0F6B1</rd:DefaultName>
          <Style>
            <Border>
              <Color>#e5e5e5</Color>
              <Style>Solid</Style>
            </Border>
            <PaddingLeft>2pt</PaddingLeft>
            <PaddingRight>2pt</PaddingRight>
            <PaddingTop>2pt</PaddingTop>
            <PaddingBottom>2pt</PaddingBottom>
          </Style>
        </Textbox>
      </CellContents>
    </TablixCell>
    <TablixCell>
      <CellContents>
        <Textbox
Name="TBReleaseDate_5A18E38F_A8C7_0F71_6FEC_AE3AC8370276">
          <CanGrow>true</CanGrow>
          <KeepTogether>true</KeepTogether>
          <Paragraphs>
            <Paragraph>
```

```xml
          <TextRuns>
           <TextRun>
            <Value>=Fields!ReleaseDate.Value</Value>
            <Style>
             <FontFamily>Tahoma</FontFamily>
             <Color>#4d4d4d</Color>
            </Style>
           </TextRun>
          </TextRuns>
          <Style />
         </Paragraph>
        </Paragraphs>

<rd:DefaultName>TBReleaseDate__5A18E38F__A8C7__0F71__6FEC__AE3AC8370276</rd:DefaultName>
         <Style>
          <Border>
           <Color>#e5e5e5</Color>
           <Style>Solid</Style>
          </Border>
          <PaddingLeft>2pt</PaddingLeft>
          <PaddingRight>2pt</PaddingRight>
          <PaddingTop>2pt</PaddingTop>
          <PaddingBottom>2pt</PaddingBottom>
         </Style>
        </Textbox>
       </CellContents>
      </TablixCell>
      <TablixCell>
       <CellContents>
        <Textbox
Name="TBSerialNumber__5C1AE86E__EECF__A723__B9B2__3A81599F9CB4">
         <CanGrow>true</CanGrow>
         <KeepTogether>true</KeepTogether>
         <Paragraphs>
          <Paragraph>
           <TextRuns>
            <TextRun>
             <Value>=Fields!SerialNumber.Value</Value>
             <Style>
              <FontFamily>Tahoma</FontFamily>
              <Color>#4d4d4d</Color>
             </Style>
            </TextRun>
           </TextRuns>
           <Style />
          </Paragraph>
         </Paragraphs>
```

```xml
<rd:DefaultName>TBSerialNumber_5C1AE86E_EECF_A723_B9B2_3A81599F9CB4</rd:DefaultName>
              <Style>
               <Border>
                <Color>#e5e5e5</Color>
                <Style>Solid</Style>
               </Border>
               <PaddingLeft>2pt</PaddingLeft>
               <PaddingRight>2pt</PaddingRight>
               <PaddingTop>2pt</PaddingTop>
               <PaddingBottom>2pt</PaddingBottom>
              </Style>
             </Textbox>
            </CellContents>
           </TablixCell>
           <TablixCell>
            <CellContents>
             <Textbox
Name="TBSMBIOSBIOSVersion_9F466916_2FA5_17CE_DDDA_FF0780C5290C">
                 <CanGrow>true</CanGrow>
                 <KeepTogether>true</KeepTogether>
                 <Paragraphs>
                  <Paragraph>
                   <TextRuns>
                    <TextRun>
                     <Value>=Fields!SMBIOSBIOSVersion.Value</Value>
                     <Style>
                      <FontFamily>Tahoma</FontFamily>
                      <Color>#4d4d4d</Color>
                     </Style>
                    </TextRun>
                   </TextRuns>
                   <Style />
                  </Paragraph>
                 </Paragraphs>

<rd:DefaultName>TBSMBIOSBIOSVersion_9F466916_2FA5_17CE_DDDA_FF0780C5290C</rd:DefaultName>
              <Style>
               <Border>
                <Color>#e5e5e5</Color>
                <Style>Solid</Style>
               </Border>
               <PaddingLeft>2pt</PaddingLeft>
               <PaddingRight>2pt</PaddingRight>
               <PaddingTop>2pt</PaddingTop>
               <PaddingBottom>2pt</PaddingBottom>
              </Style>
             </Textbox>
```

```
          </CellContents>
        </TablixCell>
        <TablixCell>
          <CellContents>
            <Textbox
Name="TBSMBIOSMajorVersion_A180070C_25FF_00B1_8D84_EE64F39F2B43">
              <CanGrow>true</CanGrow>
              <KeepTogether>true</KeepTogether>
              <Paragraphs>
                <Paragraph>
                  <TextRuns>
                    <TextRun>
                      <Value>=Fields!SMBIOSMajorVersion.Value</Value>
                      <Style>
                        <FontFamily>Tahoma</FontFamily>
                        <Color>#4d4d4d</Color>
                      </Style>
                    </TextRun>
                  </TextRuns>
                  <Style />
                </Paragraph>
              </Paragraphs>

<rd:DefaultName>TBSMBIOSMajorVersion_A180070C_25FF_00B1_8D84_EE64F39
F2B43</rd:DefaultName>
              <Style>
                <Border>
                  <Color>#e5e5e5</Color>
                  <Style>Solid</Style>
                </Border>
                <PaddingLeft>2pt</PaddingLeft>
                <PaddingRight>2pt</PaddingRight>
                <PaddingTop>2pt</PaddingTop>
                <PaddingBottom>2pt</PaddingBottom>
              </Style>
            </Textbox>
          </CellContents>
        </TablixCell>
        <TablixCell>
          <CellContents>
            <Textbox
Name="TBSMBIOSMinorVersion_B5171766_53DD_E307_9519_E8A11CFB842B">
              <CanGrow>true</CanGrow>
              <KeepTogether>true</KeepTogether>
              <Paragraphs>
                <Paragraph>
                  <TextRuns>
                    <TextRun>
                      <Value>=Fields!SMBIOSMinorVersion.Value</Value>
                      <Style>
```

```
                <FontFamily>Tahoma</FontFamily>
                <Color>#4d4d4d</Color>
                </Style>
              </TextRun>
            </TextRuns>
            <Style />
          </Paragraph>
        </Paragraphs>

<rd:DefaultName>TBSMBIOSMinorVersion_B5171766_53DD_E307_9519_E8A11CFB
842B</rd:DefaultName>
          <Style>
            <Border>
              <Color>#e5e5e5</Color>
              <Style>Solid</Style>
            </Border>
            <PaddingLeft>2pt</PaddingLeft>
            <PaddingRight>2pt</PaddingRight>
            <PaddingTop>2pt</PaddingTop>
            <PaddingBottom>2pt</PaddingBottom>
          </Style>
        </Textbox>
      </CellContents>
    </TablixCell>
    <TablixCell>
      <CellContents>
        <Textbox
Name="TBSMBIOSPresent_907D9A8C_B2C2_C7CC_BCF2_CA971609D3CC">
          <CanGrow>true</CanGrow>
          <KeepTogether>true</KeepTogether>
          <Paragraphs>
            <Paragraph>
              <TextRuns>
                <TextRun>
                  <Value>=Fields!SMBIOSPresent.Value</Value>
                  <Style>
                    <FontFamily>Tahoma</FontFamily>
                    <Color>#4d4d4d</Color>
                  </Style>
                </TextRun>
              </TextRuns>
              <Style />
            </Paragraph>
          </Paragraphs>

<rd:DefaultName>TBSMBIOSPresent_907D9A8C_B2C2_C7CC_BCF2_CA971609D3C
C</rd:DefaultName>
          <Style>
            <Border>
              <Color>#e5e5e5</Color>
```

```xml
          <Style>Solid</Style>
        </Border>
        <PaddingLeft>2pt</PaddingLeft>
        <PaddingRight>2pt</PaddingRight>
        <PaddingTop>2pt</PaddingTop>
        <PaddingBottom>2pt</PaddingBottom>
      </Style>
    </Textbox>
  </CellContents>
 </TablixCell>
 <TablixCell>
  <CellContents>
   <Textbox
Name="TBSoftwareElementID_48A0A05C_C9AF_E596_B372_66FE4F23302D">
    <CanGrow>true</CanGrow>
    <KeepTogether>true</KeepTogether>
    <Paragraphs>
     <Paragraph>
      <TextRuns>
       <TextRun>
        <Value>=Fields!SoftwareElementID.Value</Value>
        <Style>
         <FontFamily>Tahoma</FontFamily>
         <Color>#4d4d4d</Color>
        </Style>
       </TextRun>
      </TextRuns>
      <Style />
     </Paragraph>
    </Paragraphs>

<rd:DefaultName>TBSoftwareElementID_48A0A05C_C9AF_E596_B372_66FE4F23
302D</rd:DefaultName>
    <Style>
     <Border>
      <Color>#e5e5e5</Color>
      <Style>Solid</Style>
     </Border>
     <PaddingLeft>2pt</PaddingLeft>
     <PaddingRight>2pt</PaddingRight>
     <PaddingTop>2pt</PaddingTop>
     <PaddingBottom>2pt</PaddingBottom>
    </Style>
   </Textbox>
  </CellContents>
 </TablixCell>
 <TablixCell>
  <CellContents>
   <Textbox
Name="TBSoftwareElementState_CD4749D4_20EF_12AC_7CB3_50018D5D9AB0">
```

```xml
<CanGrow>true</CanGrow>
<KeepTogether>true</KeepTogether>
<Paragraphs>
 <Paragraph>
  <TextRuns>
   <TextRun>
    <Value>=Fields!SoftwareElementState.Value</Value>
    <Style>
     <FontFamily>Tahoma</FontFamily>
     <Color>#4d4d4d</Color>
    </Style>
   </TextRun>
  </TextRuns>
  <Style />
 </Paragraph>
</Paragraphs>

<rd:DefaultName>TBSoftwareElementState_CD4749D4_20EF_12AC_7CB3_50018D5D9AB0</rd:DefaultName>
<Style>
 <Border>
  <Color>#e5e5e5</Color>
  <Style>Solid</Style>
 </Border>
 <PaddingLeft>2pt</PaddingLeft>
 <PaddingRight>2pt</PaddingRight>
 <PaddingTop>2pt</PaddingTop>
 <PaddingBottom>2pt</PaddingBottom>
</Style>
</Textbox>
</CellContents>
</TablixCell>
<TablixCell>
 <CellContents>
  <Textbox
Name="TBStatus_A0700E4E_A205_4BB2_1B1A_15C5282B1AF0">
   <CanGrow>true</CanGrow>
   <KeepTogether>true</KeepTogether>
   <Paragraphs>
    <Paragraph>
     <TextRuns>
      <TextRun>
       <Value>=Fields!Status.Value</Value>
       <Style>
        <FontFamily>Tahoma</FontFamily>
        <Color>#4d4d4d</Color>
       </Style>
      </TextRun>
     </TextRuns>
     <Style />
```

```xml
          </Paragraph>
        </Paragraphs>

<rd:DefaultName>TBStatus_A0700E4E_A205_4BB2_1B1A_15C5282B1AF0</rd:Defa
ultName>
          <Style>
           <Border>
            <Color>#e5e5e5</Color>
            <Style>Solid</Style>
           </Border>
           <PaddingLeft>2pt</PaddingLeft>
           <PaddingRight>2pt</PaddingRight>
           <PaddingTop>2pt</PaddingTop>
           <PaddingBottom>2pt</PaddingBottom>
          </Style>
         </Textbox>
        </CellContents>
       </TablixCell>
       <TablixCell>
        <CellContents>
         <Textbox
Name="TBTargetOperatingSystem_F5894BED_96E3_1805_8518_D579BE31634D"
>
           <CanGrow>true</CanGrow>
           <KeepTogether>true</KeepTogether>
           <Paragraphs>
            <Paragraph>
             <TextRuns>
              <TextRun>
               <Value>=Fields!TargetOperatingSystem.Value</Value>
               <Style>
                <FontFamily>Tahoma</FontFamily>
                <Color>#4d4d4d</Color>
               </Style>
              </TextRun>
             </TextRuns>
             <Style />
            </Paragraph>
           </Paragraphs>

<rd:DefaultName>TBTargetOperatingSystem_F5894BED_96E3_1805_8518_D579B
E31634D</rd:DefaultName>
           <Style>
            <Border>
             <Color>#e5e5e5</Color>
             <Style>Solid</Style>
            </Border>
            <PaddingLeft>2pt</PaddingLeft>
            <PaddingRight>2pt</PaddingRight>
            <PaddingTop>2pt</PaddingTop>
```

```
                <PaddingBottom>2pt</PaddingBottom>
              </Style>
            </Textbox>
          </CellContents>
        </TablixCell>
        <TablixCell>
          <CellContents>
            <Textbox
Name="TBVersion_3854D8DB_16A5_3A62_8F5D_A2A7E7FBB065">
              <CanGrow>true</CanGrow>
              <KeepTogether>true</KeepTogether>
              <Paragraphs>
                <Paragraph>
                  <TextRuns>
                    <TextRun>
                      <Value>=Fields!Version.Value</Value>
                      <Style>
                        <FontFamily>Tahoma</FontFamily>
                        <Color>#4d4d4d</Color>
                      </Style>
                    </TextRun>
                  </TextRuns>
                  <Style />
                </Paragraph>
              </Paragraphs>

<rd:DefaultName>TBVersion_3854D8DB_16A5_3A62_8F5D_A2A7E7FBB065</rd:D
efaultName>
              <Style>
                <Border>
                  <Color>#e5e5e5</Color>
                  <Style>Solid</Style>
                </Border>
                <PaddingLeft>2pt</PaddingLeft>
                <PaddingRight>2pt</PaddingRight>
                <PaddingTop>2pt</PaddingTop>
                <PaddingBottom>2pt</PaddingBottom>
              </Style>
            </Textbox>
          </CellContents>
        </TablixCell>
      </TablixCells>
    </TablixRow>
  </TablixRows>
</TablixBody>
<TablixColumnHierarchy>
  <TablixMembers>
    <TablixMember />
    <TablixMember />
    <TablixMember />
```

```xml
      <TablixMember />
      <TablixMember />
      <TablixMember />
      <TablixMember />
      <TablixMember />
      <TablixMember />
      <TablixMember />
      <TablixMember />
      <TablixMember />
      <TablixMember />
      <TablixMember />
      <TablixMember />
      <TablixMember />
      <TablixMember />
      <TablixMember />
      <TablixMember />
      <TablixMember />
      <TablixMember />
     </TablixMembers>
    </TablixColumnHierarchy>
    <TablixRowHierarchy>
     <TablixMembers>
      <TablixMember>
       <KeepWithGroup>After</KeepWithGroup>
      </TablixMember>
      <TablixMember>
       <Group Name="Details" />
      </TablixMember>
     </TablixMembers>
    </TablixRowHierarchy>
    <DataSetName>DataSet1</DataSetName>
    <Top>0.4in</Top>
    <Height>0.5in</Height>
    <Width>65in</Width>
    <Style>
     <Border>
      <Style>None</Style>
     </Border>
    </Style>
   </Tablix>
   <Textbox Name="ReportTitle">
    <CanGrow>true</CanGrow>
    <KeepTogether>true</KeepTogether>
    <Paragraphs>
     <Paragraph>
      <TextRuns>
       <TextRun>
        <Value>Win32__BIOS</Value>
```

```xml
      <Style>
       <FontFamily>Verdana</FontFamily>
       <FontSize>20pt</FontSize>
      </Style>
     </TextRun>
    </TextRuns>
    <Style />
   </Paragraph>
  </Paragraphs>
  <rd:WatermarkTextbox>Title</rd:WatermarkTextbox>
  <rd:DefaultName>ReportTitle</rd:DefaultName>
  <Height>0.4in</Height>
  <Width>5.5in</Width>
  <ZIndex>1</ZIndex>
  <Style>
   <Border>
    <Style>None</Style>
   </Border>
   <PaddingLeft>2pt</PaddingLeft>
   <PaddingRight>2pt</PaddingRight>
   <PaddingTop>2pt</PaddingTop>
   <PaddingBottom>2pt</PaddingBottom>
  </Style>
 </Textbox>
</ReportItems>
<Height>2.25in</Height>
<Style>
 <Border>
  <Style>None</Style>
 </Border>
</Style>
</Body>
<Width>65in</Width>
<Page>
 <PageFooter>
  <Height>0.45in</Height>
  <PrintOnFirstPage>true</PrintOnFirstPage>
  <PrintOnLastPage>true</PrintOnLastPage>
  <ReportItems>
   <Textbox Name="ExecutionTime">
    <CanGrow>true</CanGrow>
    <KeepTogether>true</KeepTogether>
    <Paragraphs>
     <Paragraph>
      <TextRuns>
       <TextRun>
        <Value>=Globals!ExecutionTime</Value>
        <Style />
       </TextRun>
      </TextRuns>
```

```xml
        <Style>
          <TextAlign>Right</TextAlign>
          </Style>
         </Paragraph>
        </Paragraphs>
        <rd:DefaultName>ExecutionTime</rd:DefaultName>
        <Top>0.2in</Top>
        <Left>4in</Left>
        <Height>0.25in</Height>
        <Width>2in</Width>
        <Style>
          <Border>
            <Style>None</Style>
          </Border>
          <PaddingLeft>2pt</PaddingLeft>
          <PaddingRight>2pt</PaddingRight>
          <PaddingTop>2pt</PaddingTop>
          <PaddingBottom>2pt</PaddingBottom>
        </Style>
       </Textbox>
      </ReportItems>
      <Style>
        <Border>
          <Style>None</Style>
        </Border>
       </Style>
      </PageFooter>
      <LeftMargin>1in</LeftMargin>
      <RightMargin>1in</RightMargin>
      <TopMargin>1in</TopMargin>
      <BottomMargin>1in</BottomMargin>
      <Style />
     </Page>
   </ReportSection>
 </ReportSections>
 <rd:ReportUnitType>Inch</rd:ReportUnitType>
 <rd:ReportID>8514210b-15e3-4e02-8926-6584cb27ba07</rd:ReportID>
 </Report>
```

The output:

Win32_BIOS

BaseManagedEntityId	BiosCharacteristics
4fe6e1fa-3254-d6ba-3949-bce6b0fa1990	7, 11, 12, 15, 16, 17, 19, 23, 24, 25, 26, 27, 28, 29, 32, 33, 40, 42, 43, 50, 57, 58, 64, 65, 66, 67, 68, 69, 70, 71, 72, 73, 74, 75, 76, 77, 78, 79

This is the normal report from the same table:

Base Managed Entity Id	Object Status 4AE3E5FE BC03 1336 0A45 80BF58DEE 57B	Name DA5532A5 165C F1F5 BE68 4F53C316B FBD	Status A0700E4E A205 4BB2 1B1A 15C5282B1 AF0	SMBIOSBIO SVersion 9F466916 2FA5 17CE DDDA FF0780C52 90C	Other Target OS 1231CCF1 5077 39A0 D336 59EAAEC48 5DD	Manufactur er 53B4B96F C3BB 87B5 2B6F 7C6416E39 EAA	Description 59FBC381 993C 29F3 2192 BBA90136E 14A	BIOSVersio n 41F7989B ADD1 41F7 DFBB 323026333 7D3	Installable Languages FB97773A 9188 8A33 9485 E974F3208 7E8
4fe6e1fe-3254-d6ba-3949-bce6b0fa1990	acdcedb7-100c-8c91-d664-4629a218bd94	BIOS Date: 04/15/16 08:59:39 Ver: 04.06.05	OK	0901		American Megatrends Inc.	BIOS Date: 04/15/16 08:59:39 Ver: 04.06.05	ALASKA - 1072009, BIOS Date: 04/15/16 08:59:39 Ver: 04.06.05, BIOS Date: 04/15/16 08:59:39 Ver: 04.06.05	8

The HTML Report

Hello diversity

To say I have a dislike for SRS reports is an understatement. Not only are they ugly, they just don't have any flexibility.

While the single row Horizontal doesn't look much better:

Win32_BIOS

BaseManagedEntityId	BiosCharacteristics
4fe6e1fe-3254-d6ba-3949-bce6b0fa1990	7, 11, 12, 15, 16, 17, 19, 23, 24, 25, 26, 27, 28, 29, 32, 33, 40, 42, 43, 50, 57, 58, 64, 65, 66, 67, 68, 69, 70, 71, 72, 73, 74, 75, 76, 77, 78, 79 .

The single row vertical does:

Win32_BIOS

BaseManagedEntityId	4fe6e1fe-3254-d6ba-3949-bce6b0fa1990
BiosCharacteristics	7, 11, 12, 15, 16, 17, 19, 23, 24, 25, 26, 27, 28, 29, 32, 33, 40, 42, 43, 50, 57, 58, 64, 65, 66, 67, 68, 69, 70, 71, 72, 73, 74, 75, 76, 77, 78, 79
BIOSVersion	ALASKA - 1072009, BIOS Date: 04/15/16 08:59:39 Ver: 04.06.05, BIOS Date: 04/15/16 08:59:39 Ver: 04.06.05
Caption	BIOS Date: 04/15/16 08:59:39 Ver: 04.06.05
CurrentLanguage	en|US|iso8859-1
Description	BIOS Date: 04/15/16 08:59:39 Ver: 04.06.05

And there you have it. When all of this is automated, you have one heck of a program that not only creates the Management Pack dynamically, it will also create an SRS Report, or an alternative HTML Report.

Stylesheets

Decorating your reports with flair

BELOW ARE SOME STYLESHEETS I COOKED UP THAT I LIKE AND THINK YOU MIGHT, AS WELL. Don't worry I won't be offended if you take and modify to your hearts delight. In fact, please do!

NONE

```
txtstream.WriteLine("<style type='text/css'>")
txtstream.WriteLine("th")
txtstream.WriteLine("{")
txtstream.WriteLine("    COLOR: white;")
txtstream.WriteLine("}")
txtstream.WriteLine("td")
txtstream.WriteLine("{")
txtstream.WriteLine("    COLOR: white;")
txtstream.WriteLine("}")
txtstream.WriteLine("</style>")
```

BLACK AND WHITE TEXT

```
txtstream.WriteLine("<style type='text/css'>")
txtstream.WriteLine("th")
txtstream.WriteLine("{")
txtstream.WriteLine("    COLOR: white;")
txtstream.WriteLine("    BACKGROUND-COLOR: black;")
txtstream.WriteLine("    FONT-FAMILY:font-family: Cambria, serif;")
txtstream.WriteLine("    FONT-SIZE: 12px;")
txtstream.WriteLine("    text-align: left;")
txtstream.WriteLine("    white-Space: nowrap;")
txtstream.WriteLine("}")
txtstream.WriteLine("td")
txtstream.WriteLine("{")
txtstream.WriteLine("    COLOR: white;")
txtstream.WriteLine("    BACKGROUND-COLOR: black;")
txtstream.WriteLine("    FONT-FAMILY: font-family: Cambria, serif;")
txtstream.WriteLine("    FONT-SIZE: 12px;")
txtstream.WriteLine("    text-align: left;")
txtstream.WriteLine("    white-Space: nowrap;")
txtstream.WriteLine("}")
txtstream.WriteLine("div")
txtstream.WriteLine("{")
txtstream.WriteLine("    COLOR: white;")
txtstream.WriteLine("    BACKGROUND-COLOR: black;")
txtstream.WriteLine("    FONT-FAMILY: font-family: Cambria, serif;")
txtstream.WriteLine("    FONT-SIZE: 10px;")
txtstream.WriteLine("    text-align: left;")
txtstream.WriteLine("    white-Space: nowrap;")
txtstream.WriteLine("}")
txtstream.WriteLine("span")
txtstream.WriteLine("{")
txtstream.WriteLine("    COLOR: white;")
txtstream.WriteLine("    BACKGROUND-COLOR: black;")
txtstream.WriteLine("    FONT-FAMILY: font-family: Cambria, serif;")
```

```
txtstream.WriteLine("    FONT-SIZE: 10px;")
txtstream.WriteLine("    text-align: left;")
txtstream.WriteLine("    white-Space: nowrap;")
txtstream.WriteLine("    display:inline-block;")
txtstream.WriteLine("    width: 100%;")
txtstream.WriteLine("}")
txtstream.WriteLine("textarea")
txtstream.WriteLine("{")
txtstream.WriteLine("    COLOR: white;")
txtstream.WriteLine("    BACKGROUND-COLOR: black;")
txtstream.WriteLine("    FONT-FAMILY: font-family: Cambria, serif;")
txtstream.WriteLine("    FONT-SIZE: 10px;")
txtstream.WriteLine("    text-align: left;")
txtstream.WriteLine("    white-Space: nowrap;")
txtstream.WriteLine("    width: 100%;")
txtstream.WriteLine("}")
txtstream.WriteLine("select")
txtstream.WriteLine("{")
txtstream.WriteLine("    COLOR: white;")
txtstream.WriteLine("    BACKGROUND-COLOR: black;")
txtstream.WriteLine("    FONT-FAMILY: font-family: Cambria, serif;")
txtstream.WriteLine("    FONT-SIZE: 10px;")
txtstream.WriteLine("    text-align: left;")
txtstream.WriteLine("    white-Space: nowrap;")
txtstream.WriteLine("    width: 100%;")
txtstream.WriteLine("}")
txtstream.WriteLine("input")
txtstream.WriteLine("{")
txtstream.WriteLine("    COLOR: white;")
txtstream.WriteLine("    BACKGROUND-COLOR: black;")
txtstream.WriteLine("    FONT-FAMILY: font-family: Cambria, serif;")
txtstream.WriteLine("    FONT-SIZE: 12px;")
txtstream.WriteLine("    text-align: left;")
```

```
txtstream.WriteLine("    display:table-cell;")
txtstream.WriteLine("    white-Space: nowrap;")
txtstream.WriteLine("}")
txtstream.WriteLine("h1 {")
txtstream.WriteLine("color: antiquewhite;")
txtstream.WriteLine("text-shadow: 1px 1px 1px black;")
txtstream.WriteLine("padding: 3px;")
txtstream.WriteLine("text-align: center;")
txtstream.WriteLine("box-shadow: inset 2px 2px 5px rgba(0,0,0,0.5), inset -2px -2px 5px rgba(255,255,255,0.5);")
txtstream.WriteLine("}")
txtstream.WriteLine("</style>")
```

COLORED TEXT

```
txtstream.WriteLine("<style type='text/css'>")
txtstream.WriteLine("th")
txtstream.WriteLine("{")
txtstream.WriteLine("    COLOR: darkred;")
txtstream.WriteLine("    BACKGROUND-COLOR: #eeeeee;")
txtstream.WriteLine("    FONT-FAMILY:font-family: Cambria, serif;")
txtstream.WriteLine("    FONT-SIZE: 12px;")
txtstream.WriteLine("    text-align: left;")
txtstream.WriteLine("    white-Space: nowrap;")
txtstream.WriteLine("}")
txtstream.WriteLine("td")
txtstream.WriteLine("{")
txtstream.WriteLine("    COLOR: navy;")
txtstream.WriteLine("    BACKGROUND-COLOR: #eeeeee;")
txtstream.WriteLine("    FONT-FAMILY: font-family: Cambria, serif;")
txtstream.WriteLine("    FONT-SIZE: 12px;")
txtstream.WriteLine("    text-align: left;")
txtstream.WriteLine("    white-Space: nowrap;")
```

```
txtstream.WriteLine("}")
txtstream.WriteLine("div")
txtstream.WriteLine("{")
txtstream.WriteLine("    COLOR: white;")
txtstream.WriteLine("    BACKGROUND-COLOR: navy;")
txtstream.WriteLine("    FONT-FAMILY: font-family: Cambria, serif;")
txtstream.WriteLine("    FONT-SIZE: 10px;")
txtstream.WriteLine("    text-align: left;")
txtstream.WriteLine("    white-Space: nowrap;")
txtstream.WriteLine("}")
txtstream.WriteLine("span")
txtstream.WriteLine("{")
txtstream.WriteLine("    COLOR: white;")
txtstream.WriteLine("    BACKGROUND-COLOR: navy;")
txtstream.WriteLine("    FONT-FAMILY: font-family: Cambria, serif;")
txtstream.WriteLine("    FONT-SIZE: 10px;")
txtstream.WriteLine("    text-align: left;")
txtstream.WriteLine("    white-Space: nowrap;")
txtstream.WriteLine("    display:inline-block;")
txtstream.WriteLine("    width: 100%;")
txtstream.WriteLine("}")
txtstream.WriteLine("textarea")
txtstream.WriteLine("{")
txtstream.WriteLine("    COLOR: white;")
txtstream.WriteLine("    BACKGROUND-COLOR: navy;")
txtstream.WriteLine("    FONT-FAMILY: font-family: Cambria, serif;")
txtstream.WriteLine("    FONT-SIZE: 10px;")
txtstream.WriteLine("    text-align: left;")
txtstream.WriteLine("    white-Space: nowrap;")
txtstream.WriteLine("    width: 100%;")
txtstream.WriteLine("}")
txtstream.WriteLine("select")
txtstream.WriteLine("{")
```

```
txtstream.WriteLine("   COLOR: white;")
txtstream.WriteLine("   BACKGROUND-COLOR: navy;")
txtstream.WriteLine("   FONT-FAMILY: font-family: Cambria, serif;")
txtstream.WriteLine("   FONT-SIZE: 10px;")
txtstream.WriteLine("   text-align: left;")
txtstream.WriteLine("   white-Space: nowrap;")
txtstream.WriteLine("   width: 100%;")
txtstream.WriteLine("}")
txtstream.WriteLine("input")
txtstream.WriteLine("{")
txtstream.WriteLine("   COLOR: white;")
txtstream.WriteLine("   BACKGROUND-COLOR: navy;")
txtstream.WriteLine("   FONT-FAMILY: font-family: Cambria, serif;")
txtstream.WriteLine("   FONT-SIZE: 12px;")
txtstream.WriteLine("   text-align: left;")
txtstream.WriteLine("   display:table-cell;")
txtstream.WriteLine("   white-Space: nowrap;")
txtstream.WriteLine("}")
txtstream.WriteLine("h1 {")
txtstream.WriteLine("color: antiquewhite;")
txtstream.WriteLine("text-shadow: 1px 1px 1px black;")
txtstream.WriteLine("padding: 3px;")
txtstream.WriteLine("text-align: center;")
txtstream.WriteLine("box-shadow: inset 2px 2px 5px rgba(0,0,0,0.5), inset -
2px -2px 5px rgba(255,255,255,0.5);")
txtstream.WriteLine("}")
txtstream.WriteLine("</style>")
```

OSCILLATING ROW COLORS

```
txtstream.WriteLine("<style>")
```

```
txtstream.WriteLine("th")
txtstream.WriteLine("{")
txtstream.WriteLine("    COLOR: white;")
txtstream.WriteLine("    BACKGROUND-COLOR: navy;")
txtstream.WriteLine("    FONT-FAMILY:font-family: Cambria, serif;")
txtstream.WriteLine("    FONT-SIZE: 12px;")
txtstream.WriteLine("    text-align: left;")
txtstream.WriteLine("    white-Space: nowrap;")
txtstream.WriteLine("}")
txtstream.WriteLine("td")
txtstream.WriteLine("{")
txtstream.WriteLine("    COLOR: navy;")
txtstream.WriteLine("    FONT-FAMILY: font-family: Cambria, serif;")
txtstream.WriteLine("    FONT-SIZE: 12px;")
txtstream.WriteLine("    text-align: left;")
txtstream.WriteLine("    white-Space: nowrap;")
txtstream.WriteLine("}")
txtstream.WriteLine("div")
txtstream.WriteLine("{")
txtstream.WriteLine("    COLOR: navy;")
txtstream.WriteLine("    FONT-FAMILY: font-family: Cambria, serif;")
txtstream.WriteLine("    FONT-SIZE: 12px;")
txtstream.WriteLine("    text-align: left;")
txtstream.WriteLine("    white-Space: nowrap;")
txtstream.WriteLine("}")
txtstream.WriteLine("span")
txtstream.WriteLine("{")
txtstream.WriteLine("    COLOR: navy;")
txtstream.WriteLine("    FONT-FAMILY: font-family: Cambria, serif;")
txtstream.WriteLine("    FONT-SIZE: 12px;")
txtstream.WriteLine("    text-align: left;")
txtstream.WriteLine("    white-Space: nowrap;")
txtstream.WriteLine("    width: 100%;")
```

```
txtstream.WriteLine("}")
txtstream.WriteLine("textarea")
txtstream.WriteLine("{")
txtstream.WriteLine("   COLOR: navy;")
txtstream.WriteLine("   FONT-FAMILY: font-family: Cambria, serif;")
txtstream.WriteLine("   FONT-SIZE: 12px;")
txtstream.WriteLine("   text-align: left;")
txtstream.WriteLine("   white-Space: nowrap;")
txtstream.WriteLine("   display:inline-block;")
txtstream.WriteLine("   width: 100%;")
txtstream.WriteLine("}")
txtstream.WriteLine("select")
txtstream.WriteLine("{")
txtstream.WriteLine("   COLOR: navy;")
txtstream.WriteLine("   FONT-FAMILY: font-family: Cambria, serif;")
txtstream.WriteLine("   FONT-SIZE: 10px;")
txtstream.WriteLine("   text-align: left;")
txtstream.WriteLine("   white-Space: nowrap;")
txtstream.WriteLine("   display:inline-block;")
txtstream.WriteLine("   width: 100%;")
txtstream.WriteLine("}")
txtstream.WriteLine("input")
txtstream.WriteLine("{")
txtstream.WriteLine("   COLOR: navy;")
txtstream.WriteLine("   FONT-FAMILY: font-family: Cambria, serif;")
txtstream.WriteLine("   FONT-SIZE: 12px;")
txtstream.WriteLine("   text-align: left;")
txtstream.WriteLine("   display:table-cell;")
txtstream.WriteLine("   white-Space: nowrap;")
txtstream.WriteLine("}")
txtstream.WriteLine("h1 {")
txtstream.WriteLine("color: antiquewhite;")
txtstream.WriteLine("text-shadow: 1px 1px 1px black;")
```

```
txtstream.WriteLine("padding: 3px;")
txtstream.WriteLine("text-align: center;")
txtstream.WriteLine("box-shadow: inset 2px 2px 5px rgba(0,0,0,0.5), inset -2px -2px 5px rgba(255,255,255,0.5);")
txtstream.WriteLine("}")
txtstream.WriteLine("tr:nth-child(even){background-color:#f2f2f2;}")
txtstream.WriteLine("tr:nth-child(odd){background-color:#cccccc; color:#f2f2f2;}")
txtstream.WriteLine("</style>")
```

GHOST DECORATED

```
txtstream.WriteLine("<style type='text/css'>")
txtstream.WriteLine("th")
txtstream.WriteLine("{")
txtstream.WriteLine("   COLOR: black;")
txtstream.WriteLine("   BACKGROUND-COLOR: white;")
txtstream.WriteLine("   FONT-FAMILY:font-family: Cambria, serif;")
txtstream.WriteLine("   FONT-SIZE: 12px;")
txtstream.WriteLine("   text-align: left;")
txtstream.WriteLine("   white-Space: nowrap;")
txtstream.WriteLine("}")
txtstream.WriteLine("td")
txtstream.WriteLine("{")
txtstream.WriteLine("   COLOR: black;")
txtstream.WriteLine("   BACKGROUND-COLOR: white;")
txtstream.WriteLine("   FONT-FAMILY: font-family: Cambria, serif;")
txtstream.WriteLine("   FONT-SIZE: 12px;")
txtstream.WriteLine("   text-align: left;")
txtstream.WriteLine("   white-Space: nowrap;")
txtstream.WriteLine("}")
txtstream.WriteLine("div")
txtstream.WriteLine("{")
```

```
txtstream.WriteLine("   COLOR: black;")
txtstream.WriteLine("   BACKGROUND-COLOR: white;")
txtstream.WriteLine("   FONT-FAMILY: font-family: Cambria, serif;")
txtstream.WriteLine("   FONT-SIZE: 10px;")
txtstream.WriteLine("   text-align: left;")
txtstream.WriteLine("   white-Space: nowrap;")
txtstream.WriteLine("}")
txtstream.WriteLine("span")
txtstream.WriteLine("{")
txtstream.WriteLine("   COLOR: black;")
txtstream.WriteLine("   BACKGROUND-COLOR: white;")
txtstream.WriteLine("   FONT-FAMILY: font-family: Cambria, serif;")
txtstream.WriteLine("   FONT-SIZE: 10px;")
txtstream.WriteLine("   text-align: left;")
txtstream.WriteLine("   white-Space: nowrap;")
txtstream.WriteLine("   display:inline-block;")
txtstream.WriteLine("   width: 100%;")
txtstream.WriteLine("}")
txtstream.WriteLine("textarea")
txtstream.WriteLine("{")
txtstream.WriteLine("   COLOR: black;")
txtstream.WriteLine("   BACKGROUND-COLOR: white;")
txtstream.WriteLine("   FONT-FAMILY: font-family: Cambria, serif;")
txtstream.WriteLine("   FONT-SIZE: 10px;")
txtstream.WriteLine("   text-align: left;")
txtstream.WriteLine("   white-Space: nowrap;")
txtstream.WriteLine("   width: 100%;")
txtstream.WriteLine("}")
txtstream.WriteLine("select")
txtstream.WriteLine("{")
txtstream.WriteLine("   COLOR: black;")
txtstream.WriteLine("   BACKGROUND-COLOR: white;")
txtstream.WriteLine("   FONT-FAMILY: font-family: Cambria, serif;")
```

```
txtstream.WriteLine("    FONT-SIZE: 10px;")
txtstream.WriteLine("    text-align: left;")
txtstream.WriteLine("    white-Space: nowrap;")
txtstream.WriteLine("    width: 100%;")
txtstream.WriteLine("}")
txtstream.WriteLine("input")
txtstream.WriteLine("{")
txtstream.WriteLine("    COLOR: black;")
txtstream.WriteLine("    BACKGROUND-COLOR: white;")
txtstream.WriteLine("    FONT-FAMILY: font-family: Cambria, serif;")
txtstream.WriteLine("    FONT-SIZE: 12px;")
txtstream.WriteLine("    text-align: left;")
txtstream.WriteLine("    display:table-cell;")
txtstream.WriteLine("    white-Space: nowrap;")
txtstream.WriteLine("}")
txtstream.WriteLine("h1 {")
txtstream.WriteLine("color: antiquewhite;")
txtstream.WriteLine("text-shadow: 1px 1px 1px black;")
txtstream.WriteLine("padding: 3px;")
txtstream.WriteLine("text-align: center;")
txtstream.WriteLine("box-shadow: inset 2px 2px 5px rgba(0,0,0,0.5), inset -2px -2px 5px rgba(255,255,255,0.5);")
txtstream.WriteLine("}")
txtstream.WriteLine("</style>")
```

3D

```
txtstream.WriteLine("<style type='text/css'>")
txtstream.WriteLine("body")
txtstream.WriteLine("{")
txtstream.WriteLine("    PADDING-RIGHT: 0px;")
txtstream.WriteLine("    PADDING-LEFT: 0px;")
```

```
txtstream.WriteLine("    PADDING-BOTTOM: 0px;")
txtstream.WriteLine("    MARGIN: 0px;")
txtstream.WriteLine("    COLOR: #333;")
txtstream.WriteLine("    PADDING-TOP: 0px;")
txtstream.WriteLine("    FONT-FAMILY: verdana, arial, helvetica, sans-serif;")
txtstream.WriteLine("}")
txtstream.WriteLine("table")
txtstream.WriteLine("{")
txtstream.WriteLine("    BORDER-RIGHT: #999999 3px solid;")
txtstream.WriteLine("    PADDING-RIGHT: 6px;")
txtstream.WriteLine("    PADDING-LEFT: 6px;")
txtstream.WriteLine("    FONT-WEIGHT: Bold;")
txtstream.WriteLine("    FONT-SIZE: 14px;")
txtstream.WriteLine("    PADDING-BOTTOM: 6px;")
txtstream.WriteLine("    COLOR: Peru;")
txtstream.WriteLine("    LINE-HEIGHT: 14px;")
txtstream.WriteLine("    PADDING-TOP: 6px;")
txtstream.WriteLine("    BORDER-BOTTOM: #999 1px solid;")
txtstream.WriteLine("    BACKGROUND-COLOR: #eeeeee;")
txtstream.WriteLine("    FONT-FAMILY: verdana, arial, helvetica, sans-serif;")
txtstream.WriteLine("    FONT-SIZE: 12px;")
txtstream.WriteLine("}")
txtstream.WriteLine("th")
txtstream.WriteLine("{")
txtstream.WriteLine("    BORDER-RIGHT: #999999 3px solid;")
txtstream.WriteLine("    PADDING-RIGHT: 6px;")
txtstream.WriteLine("    PADDING-LEFT: 6px;")
txtstream.WriteLine("    FONT-WEIGHT: Bold;")
txtstream.WriteLine("    FONT-SIZE: 14px;")
txtstream.WriteLine("    PADDING-BOTTOM: 6px;")
txtstream.WriteLine("    COLOR: darkred;")
txtstream.WriteLine("    LINE-HEIGHT: 14px;")
txtstream.WriteLine("    PADDING-TOP: 6px;")
```

```
txtstream.WriteLine("   BORDER-BOTTOM: #999 1px solid;")
txtstream.WriteLine("   BACKGROUND-COLOR: #eeeeee;")
txtstream.WriteLine("   FONT-FAMILY:font-family: Cambria, serif;")
txtstream.WriteLine("   FONT-SIZE: 12px;")
txtstream.WriteLine("   text-align: left;")
txtstream.WriteLine("   white-Space: nowrap;")
txtstream.WriteLine("}")
txtstream.WriteLine(".th")
txtstream.WriteLine("{")
txtstream.WriteLine("   BORDER-RIGHT: #999999 2px solid;")
txtstream.WriteLine("   PADDING-RIGHT: 6px;")
txtstream.WriteLine("   PADDING-LEFT: 6px;")
txtstream.WriteLine("   FONT-WEIGHT: Bold;")
txtstream.WriteLine("   PADDING-BOTTOM: 6px;")
txtstream.WriteLine("   COLOR: black;")
txtstream.WriteLine("   PADDING-TOP: 6px;")
txtstream.WriteLine("   BORDER-BOTTOM: #999 2px solid;")
txtstream.WriteLine("   BACKGROUND-COLOR: #eeeeee;")
txtstream.WriteLine("   FONT-FAMILY: font-family: Cambria, serif;")
txtstream.WriteLine("   FONT-SIZE: 10px;")
txtstream.WriteLine("   text-align: right;")
txtstream.WriteLine("   white-Space: nowrap;")
txtstream.WriteLine("}")
txtstream.WriteLine("td")
txtstream.WriteLine("{")
txtstream.WriteLine("   BORDER-RIGHT: #999999 3px solid;")
txtstream.WriteLine("   PADDING-RIGHT: 6px;")
txtstream.WriteLine("   PADDING-LEFT: 6px;")
txtstream.WriteLine("   FONT-WEIGHT: Normal;")
txtstream.WriteLine("   PADDING-BOTTOM: 6px;")
txtstream.WriteLine("   COLOR: navy;")
txtstream.WriteLine("   LINE-HEIGHT: 14px;")
txtstream.WriteLine("   PADDING-TOP: 6px;")
```

```
txtstream.WriteLine("    BORDER-BOTTOM: #999 1px solid;")
txtstream.WriteLine("    BACKGROUND-COLOR: #eeeeee;")
txtstream.WriteLine("    FONT-FAMILY: font-family: Cambria, serif;")
txtstream.WriteLine("    FONT-SIZE: 12px;")
txtstream.WriteLine("    text-align: left;")
txtstream.WriteLine("    white-Space: nowrap;")
txtstream.WriteLine("}")
txtstream.WriteLine("div")
txtstream.WriteLine("{")
txtstream.WriteLine("    BORDER-RIGHT: #999999 3px solid;")
txtstream.WriteLine("    PADDING-RIGHT: 6px;")
txtstream.WriteLine("    PADDING-LEFT: 6px;")
txtstream.WriteLine("    FONT-WEIGHT: Normal;")
txtstream.WriteLine("    PADDING-BOTTOM: 6px;")
txtstream.WriteLine("    COLOR: white;")
txtstream.WriteLine("    PADDING-TOP: 6px;")
txtstream.WriteLine("    BORDER-BOTTOM: #999 1px solid;")
txtstream.WriteLine("    BACKGROUND-COLOR: navy;")
txtstream.WriteLine("    FONT-FAMILY: font-family: Cambria, serif;")
txtstream.WriteLine("    FONT-SIZE: 10px;")
txtstream.WriteLine("    text-align: left;")
txtstream.WriteLine("    white-Space: nowrap;")
txtstream.WriteLine("}")
txtstream.WriteLine("span")
txtstream.WriteLine("{")
txtstream.WriteLine("    BORDER-RIGHT: #999999 3px solid;")
txtstream.WriteLine("    PADDING-RIGHT: 3px;")
txtstream.WriteLine("    PADDING-LEFT: 3px;")
txtstream.WriteLine("    FONT-WEIGHT: Normal;")
txtstream.WriteLine("    PADDING-BOTTOM: 3px;")
txtstream.WriteLine("    COLOR: white;")
txtstream.WriteLine("    PADDING-TOP: 3px;")
txtstream.WriteLine("    BORDER-BOTTOM: #999 1px solid;")
```

```
txtstream.WriteLine("    BACKGROUND-COLOR: navy;")
txtstream.WriteLine("    FONT-FAMILY: font-family: Cambria, serif;")
txtstream.WriteLine("    FONT-SIZE: 10px;")
txtstream.WriteLine("    text-align: left;")
txtstream.WriteLine("    white-Space: nowrap;")
txtstream.WriteLine("    display:inline-block;")
txtstream.WriteLine("    width: 100%;")
txtstream.WriteLine("}")
txtstream.WriteLine("textarea")
txtstream.WriteLine("{")
txtstream.WriteLine("    BORDER-RIGHT: #999999 3px solid;")
txtstream.WriteLine("    PADDING-RIGHT: 3px;")
txtstream.WriteLine("    PADDING-LEFT: 3px;")
txtstream.WriteLine("    FONT-WEIGHT: Normal;")
txtstream.WriteLine("    PADDING-BOTTOM: 3px;")
txtstream.WriteLine("    COLOR: white;")
txtstream.WriteLine("    PADDING-TOP: 3px;")
txtstream.WriteLine("    BORDER-BOTTOM: #999 1px solid;")
txtstream.WriteLine("    BACKGROUND-COLOR: navy;")
txtstream.WriteLine("    FONT-FAMILY: font-family: Cambria, serif;")
txtstream.WriteLine("    FONT-SIZE: 10px;")
txtstream.WriteLine("    text-align: left;")
txtstream.WriteLine("    white-Space: nowrap;")
txtstream.WriteLine("    width: 100%;")
txtstream.WriteLine("}")
txtstream.WriteLine("select")
txtstream.WriteLine("{")
txtstream.WriteLine("    BORDER-RIGHT: #999999 3px solid;")
txtstream.WriteLine("    PADDING-RIGHT: 6px;")
txtstream.WriteLine("    PADDING-LEFT: 6px;")
txtstream.WriteLine("    FONT-WEIGHT: Normal;")
txtstream.WriteLine("    PADDING-BOTTOM: 6px;")
txtstream.WriteLine("    COLOR: white;")
```

```
txtstream.WriteLine("    PADDING-TOP: 6px;")
txtstream.WriteLine("    BORDER-BOTTOM: #999 1px solid;")
txtstream.WriteLine("    BACKGROUND-COLOR: navy;")
txtstream.WriteLine("    FONT-FAMILY: font-family: Cambria, serif;")
txtstream.WriteLine("    FONT-SIZE: 10px;")
txtstream.WriteLine("    text-align: left;")
txtstream.WriteLine("    white-Space: nowrap;")
txtstream.WriteLine("    width: 100%;")
txtstream.WriteLine("}")
txtstream.WriteLine("input")
txtstream.WriteLine("{")
txtstream.WriteLine("    BORDER-RIGHT: #999999 3px solid;")
txtstream.WriteLine("    PADDING-RIGHT: 3px;")
txtstream.WriteLine("    PADDING-LEFT: 3px;")
txtstream.WriteLine("    FONT-WEIGHT: Bold;")
txtstream.WriteLine("    PADDING-BOTTOM: 3px;")
txtstream.WriteLine("    COLOR: white;")
txtstream.WriteLine("    PADDING-TOP: 3px;")
txtstream.WriteLine("    BORDER-BOTTOM: #999 1px solid;")
txtstream.WriteLine("    BACKGROUND-COLOR: navy;")
txtstream.WriteLine("    FONT-FAMILY: font-family: Cambria, serif;")
txtstream.WriteLine("    FONT-SIZE: 12px;")
txtstream.WriteLine("    text-align: left;")
txtstream.WriteLine("    display:table-cell;")
txtstream.WriteLine("    white-Space: nowrap;")
txtstream.WriteLine("    width: 100%;")
txtstream.WriteLine("}")
txtstream.WriteLine("h1 {")
txtstream.WriteLine("color: antiquewhite;")
txtstream.WriteLine("text-shadow: 1px 1px 1px black;")
txtstream.WriteLine("padding: 3px;")
txtstream.WriteLine("text-align: center;")
```

```
txtstream.WriteLine("box-shadow: inset 2px 2px 5px rgba(0,0,0,0.5), inset -
2px -2px 5px rgba(255,255,255,0.5);")
txtstream.WriteLine("}")
txtstream.WriteLine("</style>")
```

SHADOW BOX

```
txtstream.WriteLine("<style type='text/css'>")
txtstream.WriteLine("body")
txtstream.WriteLine("{")
txtstream.WriteLine("   PADDING-RIGHT: 0px;")
txtstream.WriteLine("   PADDING-LEFT: 0px;")
txtstream.WriteLine("   PADDING-BOTTOM: 0px;")
txtstream.WriteLine("   MARGIN: 0px;")
txtstream.WriteLine("   COLOR: #333;")
txtstream.WriteLine("   PADDING-TOP: 0px;")
txtstream.WriteLine("   FONT-FAMILY: verdana, arial, helvetica, sans-serif;")
txtstream.WriteLine("}")
txtstream.WriteLine("table")
txtstream.WriteLine("{")
txtstream.WriteLine("   BORDER-RIGHT: #999999 1px solid;")
txtstream.WriteLine("   PADDING-RIGHT: 1px;")
txtstream.WriteLine("   PADDING-LEFT: 1px;")
txtstream.WriteLine("   PADDING-BOTTOM: 1px;")
txtstream.WriteLine("   LINE-HEIGHT: 8px;")
txtstream.WriteLine("   PADDING-TOP: 1px;")
txtstream.WriteLine("   BORDER-BOTTOM: #999 1px solid;")
txtstream.WriteLine("   BACKGROUND-COLOR: #eeeeee;")
txtstream.WriteLine("
filter:progid:DXImageTransform.Microsoft.Shadow(color='silver',    Direction=135,
Strength=16")
txtstream.WriteLine("}")
txtstream.WriteLine("th")
```

```
txtstream.WriteLine("{")
txtstream.WriteLine("   BORDER-RIGHT: #999999 3px solid;")
txtstream.WriteLine("   PADDING-RIGHT: 6px;")
txtstream.WriteLine("   PADDING-LEFT: 6px;")
txtstream.WriteLine("   FONT-WEIGHT: Bold;")
txtstream.WriteLine("   FONT-SIZE: 14px;")
txtstream.WriteLine("   PADDING-BOTTOM: 6px;")
txtstream.WriteLine("   COLOR: darkred;")
txtstream.WriteLine("   LINE-HEIGHT: 14px;")
txtstream.WriteLine("   PADDING-TOP: 6px;")
txtstream.WriteLine("   BORDER-BOTTOM: #999 1px solid;")
txtstream.WriteLine("   BACKGROUND-COLOR: #eeeeee;")
txtstream.WriteLine("   FONT-FAMILY: font-family: Cambria, serif;")
txtstream.WriteLine("   FONT-SIZE: 12px;")
txtstream.WriteLine("   text-align: left;")
txtstream.WriteLine("   white-Space: nowrap;")
txtstream.WriteLine("}")
txtstream.WriteLine(".th")
txtstream.WriteLine("{")
txtstream.WriteLine("   BORDER-RIGHT: #999999 2px solid;")
txtstream.WriteLine("   PADDING-RIGHT: 6px;")
txtstream.WriteLine("   PADDING-LEFT: 6px;")
txtstream.WriteLine("   FONT-WEIGHT: Bold;")
txtstream.WriteLine("   PADDING-BOTTOM: 6px;")
txtstream.WriteLine("   COLOR: black;")
txtstream.WriteLine("   PADDING-TOP: 6px;")
txtstream.WriteLine("   BORDER-BOTTOM: #999 2px solid;")
txtstream.WriteLine("   BACKGROUND-COLOR: #eeeeee;")
txtstream.WriteLine("   FONT-FAMILY: font-family: Cambria, serif;")
txtstream.WriteLine("   FONT-SIZE: 10px;")
txtstream.WriteLine("   text-align: right;")
txtstream.WriteLine("   white-Space: nowrap;")
txtstream.WriteLine("}")
```

```
txtstream.WriteLine("td")
txtstream.WriteLine("{")
txtstream.WriteLine("    BORDER-RIGHT: #999999 3px solid;")
txtstream.WriteLine("    PADDING-RIGHT: 6px;")
txtstream.WriteLine("    PADDING-LEFT: 6px;")
txtstream.WriteLine("    FONT-WEIGHT: Normal;")
txtstream.WriteLine("    PADDING-BOTTOM: 6px;")
txtstream.WriteLine("    COLOR: navy;")
txtstream.WriteLine("    LINE-HEIGHT: 14px;")
txtstream.WriteLine("    PADDING-TOP: 6px;")
txtstream.WriteLine("    BORDER-BOTTOM: #999 1px solid;")
txtstream.WriteLine("    BACKGROUND-COLOR: #eeeeee;")
txtstream.WriteLine("    FONT-FAMILY: font-family: Cambria, serif;")
txtstream.WriteLine("    FONT-SIZE: 12px;")
txtstream.WriteLine("    text-align: left;")
txtstream.WriteLine("    white-Space: nowrap;")
txtstream.WriteLine("}")
txtstream.WriteLine("div")
txtstream.WriteLine("{")
txtstream.WriteLine("    BORDER-RIGHT: #999999 3px solid;")
txtstream.WriteLine("    PADDING-RIGHT: 6px;")
txtstream.WriteLine("    PADDING-LEFT: 6px;")
txtstream.WriteLine("    FONT-WEIGHT: Normal;")
txtstream.WriteLine("    PADDING-BOTTOM: 6px;")
txtstream.WriteLine("    COLOR: white;")
txtstream.WriteLine("    PADDING-TOP: 6px;")
txtstream.WriteLine("    BORDER-BOTTOM: #999 1px solid;")
txtstream.WriteLine("    BACKGROUND-COLOR: navy;")
txtstream.WriteLine("    FONT-FAMILY: font-family: Cambria, serif;")
txtstream.WriteLine("    FONT-SIZE: 10px;")
txtstream.WriteLine("    text-align: left;")
txtstream.WriteLine("    white-Space: nowrap;")
txtstream.WriteLine("}")
```

```
txtstream.WriteLine("span")
txtstream.WriteLine("{")
txtstream.WriteLine("    BORDER-RIGHT: #999999 3px solid;")
txtstream.WriteLine("    PADDING-RIGHT: 3px;")
txtstream.WriteLine("    PADDING-LEFT: 3px;")
txtstream.WriteLine("    FONT-WEIGHT: Normal;")
txtstream.WriteLine("    PADDING-BOTTOM: 3px;")
txtstream.WriteLine("    COLOR: white;")
txtstream.WriteLine("    PADDING-TOP: 3px;")
txtstream.WriteLine("    BORDER-BOTTOM: #999 1px solid;")
txtstream.WriteLine("    BACKGROUND-COLOR: navy;")
txtstream.WriteLine("    FONT-FAMILY: font-family: Cambria, serif;")
txtstream.WriteLine("    FONT-SIZE: 10px;")
txtstream.WriteLine("    text-align: left;")
txtstream.WriteLine("    white-Space: nowrap;")
txtstream.WriteLine("    display: inline-block;")
txtstream.WriteLine("    width: 100%;")
txtstream.WriteLine("}")
txtstream.WriteLine("textarea")
txtstream.WriteLine("{")
txtstream.WriteLine("    BORDER-RIGHT: #999999 3px solid;")
txtstream.WriteLine("    PADDING-RIGHT: 3px;")
txtstream.WriteLine("    PADDING-LEFT: 3px;")
txtstream.WriteLine("    FONT-WEIGHT: Normal;")
txtstream.WriteLine("    PADDING-BOTTOM: 3px;")
txtstream.WriteLine("    COLOR: white;")
txtstream.WriteLine("    PADDING-TOP: 3px;")
txtstream.WriteLine("    BORDER-BOTTOM: #999 1px solid;")
txtstream.WriteLine("    BACKGROUND-COLOR: navy;")
txtstream.WriteLine("    FONT-FAMILY: font-family: Cambria, serif;")
txtstream.WriteLine("    FONT-SIZE: 10px;")
txtstream.WriteLine("    text-align: left;")
txtstream.WriteLine("    white-Space: nowrap;")
```

```
txtstream.WriteLine("    width: 100%;")
txtstream.WriteLine("}")
txtstream.WriteLine("select")
txtstream.WriteLine("{")
txtstream.WriteLine("    BORDER-RIGHT: #999999 3px solid;")
txtstream.WriteLine("    PADDING-RIGHT: 6px;")
txtstream.WriteLine("    PADDING-LEFT: 6px;")
txtstream.WriteLine("    FONT-WEIGHT: Normal;")
txtstream.WriteLine("    PADDING-BOTTOM: 6px;")
txtstream.WriteLine("    COLOR: white;")
txtstream.WriteLine("    PADDING-TOP: 6px;")
txtstream.WriteLine("    BORDER-BOTTOM: #999 1px solid;")
txtstream.WriteLine("    BACKGROUND-COLOR: navy;")
txtstream.WriteLine("    FONT-FAMILY: font-family: Cambria, serif;")
txtstream.WriteLine("    FONT-SIZE: 10px;")
txtstream.WriteLine("    text-align: left;")
txtstream.WriteLine("    white-Space: nowrap;")
txtstream.WriteLine("    width: 100%;")
txtstream.WriteLine("}")
txtstream.WriteLine("input")
txtstream.WriteLine("{")
txtstream.WriteLine("    BORDER-RIGHT: #999999 3px solid;")
txtstream.WriteLine("    PADDING-RIGHT: 3px;")
txtstream.WriteLine("    PADDING-LEFT: 3px;")
txtstream.WriteLine("    FONT-WEIGHT: Bold;")
txtstream.WriteLine("    PADDING-BOTTOM: 3px;")
txtstream.WriteLine("    COLOR: white;")
txtstream.WriteLine("    PADDING-TOP: 3px;")
txtstream.WriteLine("    BORDER-BOTTOM: #999 1px solid;")
txtstream.WriteLine("    BACKGROUND-COLOR: navy;")
txtstream.WriteLine("    FONT-FAMILY: font-family: Cambria, serif;")
txtstream.WriteLine("    FONT-SIZE: 12px;")
txtstream.WriteLine("    text-align: left;")
```

```
txtstream.WriteLine("    display: table-cell;")
txtstream.WriteLine("    white-Space: nowrap;")
txtstream.WriteLine("    width: 100%;")
txtstream.WriteLine("}")
txtstream.WriteLine("h1 {")
txtstream.WriteLine("color: antiquewhite;")
txtstream.WriteLine("text-shadow: 1px 1px 1px black;")
txtstream.WriteLine("padding: 3px;")
txtstream.WriteLine("text-align: center;")
txtstream.WriteLine("box-shadow: inset 2px 2px 5px rgba(0,0,0,0.5), inset -2px -2px 5px rgba(255,255,255,0.5);")
txtstream.WriteLine("}")
txtstream.WriteLine("</style>")
```